TH

SE

CO

THE FISH &
SEAFOOD
COOKBOOK

CONSULTANT EDITOR

SUSANNA TEE

p

This is a Parragon Publishing Book
First published in 2005

Parragon Publishing
Queen Street House
4 Queen Street
Bath BA1 1HE, UK

ISBN: 1-40546-034-2

Printed in Indonesia

Created and produced by The Bridgewater Book Company Ltd
Project designer Anna Hunter-Downing
Project editor Tom Kitch
Illustrator Coral Mula
Commissioned photography Clive Bozzard-Hill
Home economist Philippa Vanstone

NOTES FOR THE READER

This book uses imperial, metric, or US cup measurements.
Follow the same units of measurement throughout; do not mix
imperial and metric. All spoon measurements are level:
teaspoons are assumed to be 5 ml, and tablespoons are
assumed to be 15 ml. Unless otherwise stated, milk is assumed
to be lowfat, eggs and individual vegetables such as potatoes
are medium and pepper is freshly ground black pepper.
Sufferers from liver disease and those with weakened immune
systems should never eat raw fish. Likewise, pregnant women,
nursing mothers, and young children should avoid eating fish
raw, especially larger species such as swordfish and tuna, which
tend to have high concentrations of mercury. Recipes using raw
or very lightly cooked eggs should be avoided by infants, the
elderly, pregnant women, convalescents, and anyone suffering
from an illness. The times given are an approximate guide only.
Preparation times differ according to the techniques used by
different people and the cooking times may also vary from
those given. Optional ingredients, variations, or serving
suggestions have not been included in the calculations.

PICTURE ACKNOWLEDGMENTS

The Bridgewater Book Company would like to thank
Corbis for permission to reproduce copyright material
on pages 2, 10, 12, 16, and the front cover.

CONTENTS

1 INTRODUCTION

Fish as Food 10
Nutrition 12
Choosing and Storing Fish 14
The Fish Directory 16
Preparing Fish and Shellfish 28
Cooking Fish and Shellfish 38
Preparing Sushi 42
Basic Recipes 44

2 FISH NIBBLES

Taramasalata 50
Tuna & Tomato Boreks 51
Tuna Sesame Blocks 52
Seven-Spiced Salmon Rolls 54
Pressed Sushi Bars with Smoked
   Salmon & Cucumber 55
Scattered Sushi with Smoked Mackerel 56
Seafood Tempura 59
Fish Fritters 60
Bagna Cauda 62
Devils & Angels on Horseback 63
Shrimp Wrapped in Ham 64
Sizzling Chili Shrimp 66
Sesame Shrimp Toasts 67
Deep-Fried Shrimp Balls 68
Jumbo Shrimp with Sweet & Sour Sauce 69
Mussels with Herb & Garlic Butter 70
Caribbean Crab Cakes 73
Seafood Phyllo Packages 74
Crispy Crab Won Tons 75

3 FISH FIRST

Smoked Fish Pâté 78
Tuna Stuffed Tomatoes 80
Gravadlax 81
Thai Fish Cakes 83
Noodle-Wrapped Teriyaki Fish 84
Salmon Tartare 85
Angler Fish, Rosemary & Bacon Skewers 86
Shrimp Cocktail 89
Shrimp Satay 90
Moules Marinière 91
Ceviche 92
Chevre & Oyster Tartlets 93
Scallops in Saffron Sauce 95
Potted Crab 96
Calamares 99

4 SOUPS AND STEWS

Cod & Sweet Potato Soup	102
Garlic Fish Soup	104
Breton Fish Soup with Cider & Sorrel	105
Saffron Fish Soup	106
Mexican Fish & Roasted Tomato Soup	107
Trout & Celery Root Soup	108
Thai Shrimp & Scallop Soup	109
Shrimp & Vegetable Bisque	110
Mussel Soup	113
Corn & Crab Soup	114
Haddock & Potato Soup	115
Smoked Cod Chowder	116
Caribbean Fish Chowder	117
Shrimp Laksa	118
Shrimp Gumbo	120
Bouillabaisse	121
Cioppino	122
New England Clam Chowder	124
Basque Tuna Stew	125
Chunky Cod Stew with Celery & Potatoes	127
Spanish Swordfish Stew	128
Louisiana Gumbo	130
Catalan Fish Stew	131
Brazilian Seafood Stew	133

5 LIGHT LUNCHES AND SUPPER DISHES

Kedgeree	136
Smoked Haddock & Gruyère Soufflé Tart	139
Omelet Arnold Bennett	140
Haddock Goujons	142
Salmon Frittata	143
Seafood Omelet	144
Pan Bagna	146
Fish Cakes	147

Deep-Fried Seafood	149
Fish Tacos	150
Fish & Refried Bean Tostadas	151
Fish Burritos	152
Fish & Yogurt Quenelles	153
Fresh Sardines Baked with Lemon & Oregano	154
Pissaladière	156
Linguine with Anchovies, Olives & Capers	157
Creamy Smoked Trout Tagliatelle	158
Singapore Noodles	160
Pad Thai	161
Seafood Pizza	162
Spaghetti with Clams	163
Seafood Risotto	165
Crab & Watercress Tart	166
Crab Soufflé	167

6 SALADS

Mackerel & Potato Salad	170
Smoked Haddock Salad	172
Salad Niçoise	173
Moroccan Couscous Salad	174
Warm Tuna & Kidney Bean Salad	175
Tuna & Two-Bean Salad	176
Tuna & Herbed Fusilli Salad	178
Smoked Salmon & Wild Arugula Salad	179
Smoked Salmon, Asparagus & Avocado Salad	180
Shrimp & Rice Salad	182
Chinese Shrimp Salad	184
Thai Noodle Salad with Shrimp	185
Seafood Salad	186
Seafood & Spinach Salad	188
Crab & Citrus Salsa	189
Cantaloupe & Crab Salad	191

7 HEARTY MAIN DISHES

Baked Mackerel Stuffed with Raisins & Pine Nuts	194
Salmon Coulibiac	196
Salmon Steaks with Green Sauce	197
Poached Salmon	198
Cod with Catalan Spinach	201
Flaky Pastry Fish Pie	202
Angler Fish Packages	203
Fish Curry with Rice Noodles	204
Moroccan Fish Tagine	206
Flounder for Two	207
Porgy en Papillote	208
Sole Florentine	209
Sole Meunière	210
Whole Deep-Fried Fish with Soy & Ginger	212
Skate in Black Butter Sauce	213
Hake in White Wine	214
Broiled Red Snapper with Garlic	215
Fisherman's Pie	216
Sicilian Tuna	218
Swordfish with Olives & Capers	219
Trout with Almonds	220
Trout in Lemon & Red Wine Sauce	221
Paella	223
Stuffed Squid	224

8 BARBECUES AND GRIDDLES

Herrings with Orange Tarragon Stuffing	228
Salmon Teriyaki	229
Barbecued Salmon	230
Nut-Crusted Halibut	233
Cod & Tomato Packages	234
Blackened Fish	235
Caribbean Sea Bass	236
Angler Fish Kabobs	238
Spicy Porgy	239
Indonesian Spiced Fish	241
Tuna & Tarragon Skewers	242
Barbecued Swordfish	244
Stuffed Sardines	245
Bacon-Wrapped Trout	246
Fennel-Basted Trout Fillets	248
Whole Griddled Fish	249
Shrimp & Mixed Bell Pepper Kabobs	250
Seafood Brochettes	253
Index	254

1

The Fish and Seafood Cookbook is a comprehensive guide to preparing, cooking, and serving every kind of fish and shellfish. Confirmed fish devotees will treasure having all their favorite, classic recipes in one volume, in addition to a range of new, imaginative ideas, while those who may find fish preparation rather daunting will be enlightened, reassured, and inspired.

INTRODUCTION

The Fish Directory at the front of the book introduces the fabulous wealth of healthy, delicious food that our waters— both fresh and sea—can offer. All the basic techniques for preparing and cooking these different varieties of fish and shellfish are then explained and demonstrated in detail. The collection of recipes that follows caters for every meal type and occasion, from elegant finger food to hearty main meals, and encompasses all the popular cuisines around the globe, from the Mediterranean to Mexico.

FISH AS FOOD

There are about 21,000 species of fish in the world and, perhaps surprisingly, up to 120 commercial species available to buy as food. Fish and shellfish come in all different shapes, sizes and colors, from the sea, rivers, and lakes, from cold waters and warm waters. Fish fits easily into today's lifestyle. It is light, elegant, substantial, and nutritious. Cooking fish is also quick and easy, making it a perfect fast food for busy cooks.

Not only does fish come in all shapes and sizes, it also comes whole, filleted, sliced, boned, skinned, and canned. The choice appears almost endless and, on top of that, it is available all the year round.

The range of fish and fish dishes can sometimes appear daunting, or even off-putting. However there are excellent reasons to learn more about cooking fish.

Firstly, fish is good for our bodies and souls, from head to toe. It is high in protein, vitamins, and minerals, and low in saturated fat. It's the perfect addition to our diet, keeping our hair, skin, eyes, teeth, and bones in good health. Research has also shown that eating a diet containing oil-rich fish aids a healthy heart and helps our brains to perform, leading to a longer, healthier life.

FOOD FOR THOUGHT?

Some researchers have claimed that eating oil-rich fish can boost our brain power and decrease the risk of dementia, depression, and poor memory. Just one 5 oz/140 g serving or two smaller servings of oily fish will provide a week's supply.

As well as being good for you, fish is good to eat. The huge variety of recipes, from all over the world, pay tribute to the versatility and popularity of fish as the basis for a tasty meal for all the family. In addition, selecting and cooking fish can be as simple or as complicated as you want it to be. But for those who find it difficult to know where to start, help is at hand.

This book will take you through selection, preparation, and cooking the most common types of fish and seafood.

Remember, you can also ask your local fish supplier for advice or to prepare the fish for you. This way, you can make sure that your fish will be as fresh and tasty as possible. Fish is the dish of the moment—try it and you will soon be hooked!

SEA OF ROMANCE

While it has long been considered a myth that oysters are an aphrodisiac, it is true that shellfish, and in particular oysters, contain high levels of zinc, a mineral that is important for male fertility and good health.

NUTRITION

Fish is good for you: it's official. It is an excellent source of first-class protein, low in fat in the case of white fish, low in salt, and contains varying degrees of vitamins and minerals, such as vitamins A and D in oil-rich fish, a range of the B vitamins, iron, calcium, copper, magnesium, manganese, phosphorus, potassium, selenium, sodium, iodine, fluorine, and zinc.

FISH RICH IN OMEGA-3 FATTY ACIDS

These include gray mullet, halibut, herring, kippered herring, sardine, pilchard, barracuda, mackerel, dolphin fish, eel, swordfish, salmon, trout, scallops, and tuna, but only if it is fresh, as the canning process destroys the omega-3.

HEALTH BENEFITS

Even the fat found in oil-rich fish contains high amounts of the essential polyunsaturated fats called omega-3 fatty acids. These are essential to health because they cannot be produced by the human body. Research suggests that these fatty acids reduce cholesterol absorption and help to lower cholesterol levels in the blood, which prevents the arteries from clogging and averts coronary heart diseases. Even people who have had a heart attack are advised to increase their consumption of oil-rich fish to help prevent another heart attack. There is also some evidence that these omega-3 fatty acids help in the prevention of certain cancers, such as breast, prostate, and colon cancer, as well as reducing inflammation in people suffering from rheumatoid arthritis and can even improve brain activity. These important fatty acids are found almost exclusively in oil-rich fish.

LOW IN SALT

Surprising, since most fish spend their lives in salt water!

HEART ATTACKS

Current research suggests that eating at least one portion of oil-rich fish per week, as part of a healthy diet, greatly reduces the risk of having a heart attack.

EATING RAW FISH

Fish is usually cooked before eating but, traditionally, sushi is made with both raw and cooked fish. If you make sushi with raw fish, you must realize that there is an element of risk when eating it. Raw fish is more likely to contain bacteria and parasites than cooked fish because it has not been subjected to the correct amount of heat to destroy them. All the recipes in this book can be made with cooked fish, but if you prefer to use raw fish, then be careful to follow the guidelines below:
• People suffering from certain diseases, such as liver disease, and those with weakened immune systems should not eat raw fish or shellfish.
• Only buy really fresh fish, from a reputable supplier or store that sells "sushi grade" or "sashimi grade" fish.

MERCURY LEVELS

Levels of mercury, which is found in water from naturally occurring sources and industrial pollution, tend to be higher in long-lived, larger oil-rich fish, such as mackerel, tuna, swordfish, shark, and marlin. For most people, the levels are too low to be of concern. However, pregnant women, nursing mothers, and children under 16 should not eat these types of fish, as the levels of mercury in them can be harmful to a baby's and child's development. However, oil-rich fish such as herring, sardine, pilchard, trout, and salmon are safe to eat.

TOXINS IN FISH

Although the incidence of toxin poisoning is very rare, some fish from warm waters eat a toxin in their diet and, in turn, are toxic if eaten by another fish. Fish that are particularly vulnerable include the barracuda, sturgeon, moray eel, and some snappers and groupers. The toxins build up over time in the liver, so never eat the liver of these fish, and should you suffer from an extreme headache, tingling, irritation, or a rash on the skin, weakness, or sickness, seek medical help.

CHOOSING AND STORING FISH

Fish and shellfish are best eaten really fresh, which means straight from the water or within two or three days of being caught. Fish, particularly shellfish, is extremely perishable. The solution is to purchase fish from a reputable fish supplier who has a fast turnover of produce, and this could be your local fish merchant, supermarket fish counter or chilling cabinet, delivery van, or market. Carry the fish home in a cooler bag and, if possible, plan to eat it on the day of purchase. Chilling slows down deterioration and so, due to its short storage time, many fish are cleaned or filleted and either chilled or frozen onboard fishing boats. This helps to keep the fish in prime condition.

WHICH FISH?

Some varieties of fish are available all the year round, while others are not available during, for example, spawning time. When choosing fish, be flexible and take advantage of the variety of fish on sale as many fish are interchangeable in recipes. It is the fish's fat content that is important in helping to select an alternative fish, as it is this that often determines the fish's flavor, texture, color, and cooking method. Remember too that there is a wide variety of frozen fish available.

Freshness

• The eyes should look bright, full, and clear, not sunken, cloudy, and dry. Herring's eyes should be a red color.
• The gills under the flaps on both sides of the fish's head should look bright and be pink or red in color, not gray or dark green and slimy.

• The body should be plump, stiff, and firm, and the scales tightly fitting, not limp.
• The skin should be shiny, bright colored, and moist, not faded and dull.
• The flesh should be firm and elastic and should spring back when you press it with your finger, not leave an indentation. The flesh of fillets and steaks should look freshly cut and moist with a firm texture, not dry and discolored.
• It should smell fresh and slightly of the sea air, not strongly fishy or of ammonia.
• The shells of shellfish should be undamaged and mussels, clams, and oysters should close tightly if touched.
• The tails of shrimp should curl under them.
• Select crabs by weight, not size, as a good crab should be heavy for its size, and shake the crab and reject it if any water comes from inside it.

• Frozen fish should be frozen hard with no sign of partial thawing and should be in packaging that is undamaged.

IT'S A MYTH

The saying that oysters should only be bought when there is an "r" in the month has no basis in fact as oysters are good all the year round.

STORAGE

Once you've bought your fish and got it home, unwrap it immediately, place it in a dish, then cover and store toward the bottom of the refrigerator. Shellfish should be put in a container, covered with a wet cloth, and stored in the refrigerator. If possible, eat on the day of purchase, otherwise eat within 24 hours. Ready-to-eat cooked fish, such as smoked mackerel, shrimp, and crabs, should be stored on the shelves above raw fish to avoid contamination. Smoked salmon, once the pack is opened, can be stored in the refrigerator for up to one week, but not beyond its use-by date.

If you have to store fresh fish for longer than 24 hours, freezing is the best option. Firmer-fleshed fish tend to freeze better than less firm-fleshed fish, as they retain their texture during the process. Freeze on the day of purchase and thaw overnight in the refrigerator.

HOW LONG TO FREEZE?

From a safety angle, once the fish is in the freezer it can be stored almost for ever as long as the temperature is maintained at 0°F/-18°C. However, from a food value, taste, texture, and color angle, white fish is best stored for up to 3 months and oily fish for up to 2 months.

THE FISH DIRECTORY

The following is a guide to all the main species of fish and shellfish that can be eaten, listed

by their common names, although some fish, confusingly, are known by a variety of different

names. The potted profile for each fish details the various forms in which it can be purchased,

for example whole or in fillets, fresh, and canned, and the most suitable cooking methods.

Fresh fish are classified into groups according to their features. Flatfish, which vary in size from a small flounder to a large halibut, have a flat bone structure, a dark upper skin, and white belly, their eyes face upward and they swim on their sides. Roundfish also vary in size, from a small sardine to a huge pompano, but all have long, slender, rounded bodies, eyes at the side of their head, and all swim with their dorsal fin uppermost. Both flat- and roundfish live their entire lives in the sea, whereas freshwater fish live in rivers and lakes. Exceptions are the salmon and salmon trout, which live in the sea as adults but migrate to fresh water in order to spawn, and the eel, which travels from fresh water to sea water to spawn.

Shellfish are divided into two groups: mollusks and crustaceans. Mollusks have a soft body that is encased inside one or two protective hard outer shells. The exceptions are the cephalopods, which have tentacles protruding from their head. Crustaceans have hard external shells, which are segmented to allow movement.

Fish can be preserved by canning, hot or cold smoking, salting, drying, or pickling as detailed in the Fish Directory under the relevant entry for each fish.

FLAT SEAFISH

American Plaice
One of the most popular flatfish, it is distinguished by the large red or orange spots on its brown back. It is available whole or in fillets and its white flesh can be fried, broiled, poached, steamed, or baked.

Flounder
Flounder is very similar to plaice, but its flavor and texture are not so fine. It is available whole or in fillets and can be cooked in the same way as plaice. In America, flounder is a collective name for several varieties of flatfish.

Brill
Brill is smaller but not dissimilar to turbot in flavor and texture. It is usually sold whole, but can be halved, sliced, or filleted and lends itself to being cooked by any method.

Dover Sole
This is one of the finest-flavored and fine-textured small flatfish. Its white flesh has an exquisite flavor. It is imported frozen to the the United States and is available in good markets. It is traditionally broiled, a classic recipe being Sole Meunière (see page 210).

English Sole
English sole, which is also called lemon sole, is not dissimilar to Dover sole, although it has much less flavor and its white flesh has a fine texture but is less firm. It can be purchased and cooked in the same way.

Turbot
This fish, with its huge brown, knobbly body and small head, is considered the finest of the flat fish. It is low in fat, has firm, snow-white flesh, and a fine, delicate taste. It is usually imported frozen to the United States and can be baked, poached, or steamed.

Dolphin Fish/Mahi-Mahi/Dorado
Found in warm waters, this is a stunningly attractive fish with a streamlined silver body and black and gold spots, which sadly fade once it is caught. Small fish are sold whole, whereas larger fish are sold in steaks and fillets. Its flesh is firm and well flavored, and is very versatile as it can be fried, broiled, and cooked in a pie, as in the traditional Maltese pie known as Lampuki.

Halibut
This large flatfish is available whole or as steaks or fillets. Its flesh is quite oily and its firm texture makes it suitable for baking, braising, poaching, or steaming. Halibut is also available smoked.

Sand Dab
This is one of the smallest flatfish and belongs to the flounder family. It has a rough, light brown upper skin and white flesh. It is available whole or in fillets and can be cooked in the same way as flounder.

Skate
This strange-looking fish is shaped like a kite. There are several varieties, of which only the fish's pectoral fin, known as its wings, and small pieces of flesh cut from the bony part of the fish, known as nobs, are eaten. It is low in fat and has a superior flavor. Skate can be fried, broiled, poached, or steamed, a classic dish being Skate in Black Butter Sauce (see page 213).

ROUND SEAFISH

Sea Bass/Bass
This large, sleek fish, similar in shape to salmon, has dark, silver-gray scales, which should be removed before cooking, and a white belly. Its firm, white flesh has an excellent flavor. It can be bought whole or in steaks or fillets and is suitable for poaching or steaming.

Cod
This very popular, white-fleshed fish varies enormously in size and is available whole, which is particularly suitable for baking, poaching, or steaming, and in fillets and steaks, which can be fried or broiled. It is commonly used in cooked dishes such as Fisherman's Pie (see page 216). Much of it is frozen aboard fishing boats. It is also available salted, smoked, and dried. Cod's roe is available fresh and smoked and can be used to make Taramasalata (see page 50).

Pollock/Coley/Saithe/ Coalfish
Pollock is related to the cod family and has pinkish-gray flesh that becomes white when cooked. Usually available as fillets or steaks, it can be used in the same way as cod but, as it can be dry, is not suitable for broiling. It is usually used in soups, stews, and fish pies.

Haddock
This fish has a firm, white flesh and is closely related to cod, although it is usually smaller and can be distinguished by the dark streak that runs down its back and the two black marks either side of its gills. Sold as fillets or steaks, it is interchangeable with cod in recipes and is used as an alternative when serving fish and french fries. Haddock is often smoked—it is used as such in the well-known dish Kedgeree (see page 136).

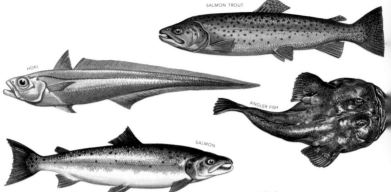

Hoki

Imported from New Zealand, hoki is related to hake, which in turn is a member of the cod family. Its white flesh is firm, contains very few bones and has a mild flavor. It is sold in fillets or pieces and can be baked, fried, or broiled.

Angler Fish/ Monkfish

This deep-sea fish has such a large, ugly head that usually only the tail is sold, boned as a whole piece or skinned and filleted. Its flesh is firm, white, and moist, which makes it very suitable for cutting into cubes for kabobs, and can be fried, broiled, baked, roasted, poached, or steamed.

Parrot Fish

This beautiful tropical fish with skin ranging in color from turquoise, green, pink, and violet and its round, beaklike face really does look like a parrot. Its flesh is white and firm and is best cooked whole.

Pomfret/Butterfish

This silver, fairly small fish from warm waters is a roundfish but, like porgy, is laterally compressed and therefore prepared as though a flatfish. The flesh is white and delicate and can be stuffed and baked whole or filleted and fried or broiled.

Tilefish

Tilefish, also called golden snapper, has a multicolored body with distinctive yellow spots and firm, pinkish white flesh. It has a very delicate flavor and is available fresh or frozen, whole, or in steaks, or fillets. Once cooked the flesh remains succulent and is excellent poached, baked, or broiled.

Salmon

Most salmon varieties mature at sea and then return to coastal rivers and streams to spawn. Atlantic salmon (wild salmon) and farmed salmon are available, and increased harvests of farmed salmon have made this popular fish more affordable. Salmon has a high-fat content and a firm flesh, which can be pink to dark red. It can be poached or baked whole and its steaks or fillets can be fried or broiled. Its red roe is available as salmon caviar, although this description only really applies to sturgeon roe. It is also popular canned and smoked. Smoked salmon is dry-salted before being smoked and is sold in fillets, which are cut into paper-thin slices.

Salmon Trout/Sea Trout

This fish is often confused with salmon as it also returns from the sea to spawn in rivers. It is smaller than salmon, but larger than trout, has pale pink flesh and can be used in the same way as salmon or trout (though salmon trout is too delicate for smoking). It can be purchased whole or as fillets.

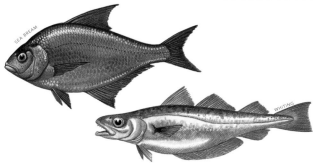

Sea Bream
There are numerous varieties of this large fish, including the red, black, white, pink, ray, and gilt-head sea bream. All have firm, white flesh, but the red bream is generally considered to have the best flavor. It is usually cooked whole and can be stuffed and baked, broiled, or braised. Their interesting story is that they start life as males and later turn into females!

Whiting
This fish, related to hake, is fairly small and has pale brown skin and a cream belly. Its flesh is white and very soft, with a bland flavor. It can be bought fresh, either whole or in fillets, as well as smoked or salted. It is suitable for frying, broiling, poaching, or steaming.

Barracuda
This large, fierce fish from warm waters has white flesh with a firm texture. Small barracuda can be filleted and are suitable for baking, frying, broiling, poaching, steaming, and for using in soups and stews. Never eat barracuda raw, or its liver, as it can be toxic (see page 13).

Gray Mullet
This fish, unrelated to the red mullet, looks and tastes similar to sea bass. It has firm, white flesh and can be bought whole or in fillets and is best baked or broiled. Its roe is traditionally used to make Taramasalata (see page 50).

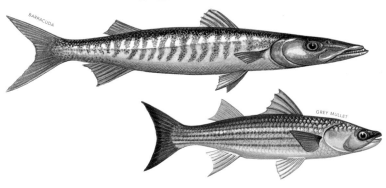

HAKE

JOHN DORY

HERRING

MACKEREL

Hake

This large fish is a member of the cod family, but has a slightly firmer, white flesh. Large hake are cut into fillets or steaks and these are usually poached, but can also be fried or broiled. Small hake are sold whole. Smoked hake is also available as well as salted hake, which is prepared and used in the same way as salt cod.

Herring

A small, very oily fish, available whole or filleted, that can be fried or broiled or stuffed and baked. Due to its oiliness, the herring is ideal for preserving. Rollmop herrings are raw herrings, boned, rolled up with chopped onions, gherkins, and peppercorns, and then marinated in spiced vinegar. Herrings are also smoked. Kippered herrings are the most popular form and are sold in fillets or whole, often in pairs. Ideally, dye is not used in the process. Buckling is another version of smoked herring and often considered the best, and there are also bloaters,

which are lightly salted, and which are also smoked herrings. Herrings are also available salted, having been preserved between layers of salt, and they are also sold canned.

John Dory/Dory

In most parts of the world, John Dory is called St Peter or St Pierre (not to be confused with St Peter's Fish). Although a roundfish, John Dory is laterally compressed so prepared as a flatfish, from which there is little flesh and lots of waste. It is usually filleted and fried.

Porgy

The most popular porgy is scup, which is found in the Atlantic. It has firm flesh with a delicate and

mild flavor. Porgy is available fresh or frozen and is generally sold whole. It is suitable for baking, broiling, and frying.

Mackerel

This fish, with its striking black markings and silver belly, is particularly oily, which makes it ideal for frying and broiling or stuffing and baking. As its dark flesh has a distinctive flavor, it is often accompanied by a sharp-flavored sauce, such as gooseberry. Mackerel is available whole or in fillets as well as canned or smoked. Smoked mackerel has a rich, strong flavor and is sold in fillets.

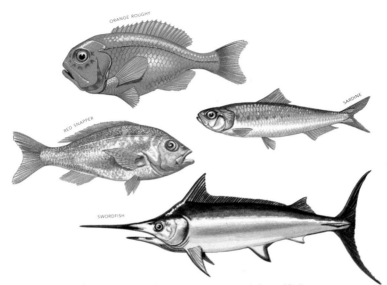

Orange Roughy

This fish is bright orange and spiny and, like hoki, is imported from New Zealand. Its flesh is snow white and dense and has a mild flavor. Its unusual feature is that it has a layer of fat beneath its skin, which is removed during filleting. It is interchangeable with cod in recipes. Available in specialty markets.

Drum

Drum belong to the croaker family and live in both fresh- and seawater. Drum are so called because of the noise it makes under the water, which resemble a muffled drum. It is generally sold in fillets and steaks and can be baked, broiled, or fried.

Red Snapper

This large fish, identified by its vivid rose-pink skin and red eyes, has white, creamy flesh and is cut into fillets or steaks, which can be fried, broiled, poached, or steamed. Small red snappers are available whole and can be stuffed and baked.

Sardine/Pilchard

These oily, strong-flavored fish vary in size. The smaller fish are called sardines, whereas the larger, mature fish are known as pilchard, three or four of which make one serving. They are sold fresh and can be fried, broiled, or baked. Sardines are also sold canned and can be eaten whole as the preserving process softens their bones.

Swordfish

Swordfish is an enormous fish and is sold as steaks or chunks. Its firm, dense texture makes it perfect for broiling and pan-frying, although it can also be poached, steamed, or baked.

Tuna

There are many species of this large fish, with its dark blue back and silver-gray sides and belly, including the skipjack, yellowfin, bluefin, albacore, and big-eye. Its flesh varies in color from pale pink to dark red and it has a high fat content and a firm, dense texture. It can be bought in chunks or steaks, which can be fried, broiled, braised, or poached, but should not be overcooked as it tends to dry out during cooking. Tuna is also sold canned in oil, brine, or water.

Pompano

This fish from warm waters has a silver skin and fatty flesh. It can be bought whole or in fillets. Its skin should be removed before cooking. It can be baked, fried, broiled, steamed, poached, or used in soups and stews.

Conger Eel/ Moray Eel

These are snakelike fish whose bodies can grow up to 8 feet/2.5 meters. It is available smoked. The moray eel, of which there are several species, are cousins of the conger eel, but much smaller. Both conger and moray eels have firm, white flesh and are usually sold in steaks. They can be roasted or baked and are good in pies, soups, and stews.

Anchovy

These small fish are identified by their large mouths, which almost stretch back to their gills. They are high in fat and, although occasionally available fresh, most are filleted, cured in salt and oil, and then canned. They are sold flat or rolled.

Lingcod

Lingcod, with its long, brown, eellike body, is the largest member of the cod family and has soft, white flesh. It is seldom available fresh, but is usually either salted or smoked.

Sprat

Sprat is now rarely sold fresh, but is available smoked. It is very similar to a small herring and can be used in the same way.

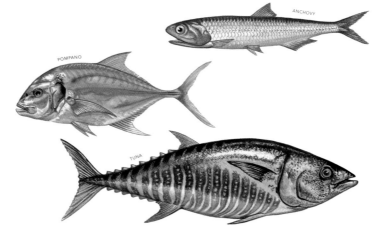

ANCHOVY

POMPANO

TUNA

FRESHWATER FISH

Catfish/Rockfish

There are many species of catfish, many of which are frozen. It is available whole or as fillets and its tough skin must be removed before cooking. It can be fried, broiled, poached, steamed, baked, or used in soups or stews.

Trout

There are many varieties of trout, including river, brown, rainbow, and salmon trout. It is usually cooked whole and can be baked, fried, broiled, poached, or steamed. It is also available smoked, in the same way as smoked salmon.

Char

Char is similar to trout in size and appearance, but more colorful. Its flesh is firm and usually white, or sometimes pale pink. Arctic char is now commonly available, thanks to farming in Iceland and Canada. It is usually sold filleted and as such can be fried, baked, or steamed.

Tilapia/ St Peter's Fish

Due to farming, tilapia is now more widely available and can be purchased whole or as fillets. It has a firm texture and is suitable for all cooking methods. An interesting feature of this fish is that the females carry their young in their mouths. They are smaller than the males.

Eel/Common Eel/Elver

This snakelike fish, smaller than the seawater conger eel, lives in rivers and streams and then swims thousands of miles to return to the sea and spawn, after which it dies (the opposite migratory habit of salmon). Elvers are baby eels and are no longer eaten, but used to restock fisheries. Killing and skinning a fresh eel is not practical at home and for this reason it is best done by your fish supplier. It can be jellied, fried, broiled, poached, stewed, or baked. Eel is also available smoked.

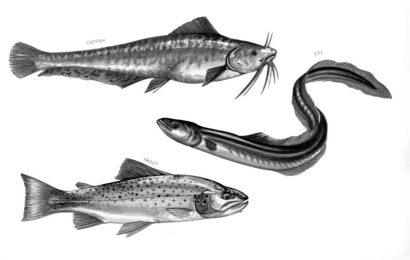

CATFISH

EEL

TROUT

Oyster

There are many varieties of this shellfish, which vary in size. The traditional way of eating them is raw, straight from the half shell with their juices. Shucked oysters are available smoked, canned, and dried.

Scallop and Bay

Scallops and bays both have ribbed fan shells, but bay scallops are smaller than scallops and are more widely available. Unlike other mollusks, scallops cannot hold their shells tightly closed and die soon after they are taken out of water. This means that they are very perishable and are often removed from their shells and iced aboard fishing boats as soon as they are caught. Both the white muscle and orange coral, or roe, are eaten and have an exquisite, delicate taste. They can be bought fresh or frozen and can be fried, broiled, or steamed.

Shrimp

There are numerous varieties of shrimp, which vary in both size and color from tiny to jumbo. They are available all year-round and can be fresh, cooked whole or shelled and frozen, canned, or dried. Some large shrimp are sometimes called prawns. A classic way of serving shrimp as an appetizer is Shrimp Cocktail (see page 89).

SHELLFISH

Clam

There are many varieties of clam, which vary in size and have either soft or hard shells. They are sold live in their shells and larger clams are steamed open, whereas smaller varieties can be eaten raw. They are also sold smoked and canned.

Mussel

Identified by their dark blue shell, mussels cling to rocks or the sea bed and take about two years to reach maturity. They are available live or frozen and are cooked by steaming, which opens their shells. The best known mussels recipe is Moules Marinière (see page 91).

CRAB

Crab

There are several varieties of this crustacean, including the blue or soft-shell crab, the common crab, the green or shore crab, and the spider crab. Crab can be bought alive, uncooked in the shell, cooked, with or without the shell, fresh, and canned. Its flesh consists of both white meat, found in the claws and legs, and brown meat, found in the body. Crab can be baked, steamed, or boiled. Fresh crab can also be purchased "dressed," with the meat arranged attractively in the shell ready for eating. Canned dressed crab is also available.

Lobster

Lobster, considered by some to be the finest crustacean, can take seven years to reach marketable size. There are several varieties and they can be bought live, when dark blue, or cooked in the shell, when the lobster turns bright pink. Lobster can also be purchased frozen whole or as frozen tails and canned. It can be baked, boiled, steamed, or broiled.

Dublin Bay Prawn/ Langoustine/Norway Lobster/Scampi

This attractive shellfish looks like a miniature version of a lobster. It is available live or cooked, with its shell or shelled. When shelled and coated in bread crumbs, it is known as scampi.

Rock Lobster/ Spiny Lobster

This is another shellfish that looks similar to a small lobster. It is prepared and cooked in the same way as lobster.

Freshwater Crayfish/ Crawfish

Called crawfish in the South, it also resembles a tiny lobster. These are the only shellfish found in fresh waters.

Octopus

The octopus is a cephalopod and has eight tentacles. It varies in size and large ones—as large as 10 feet/3 meters—are available prepared in pieces and small ones are available whole. Octopus can be poached or used in soups and stews.

Squid

The squid, of which there are several varieties varying in size, is a cephalopod and has ten tentacles. The tentacles are chopped and the body either sliced or kept whole and stuffed. Large squid are usually stewed and small squid can be fried, broiled, or poached. Its ink, found in a sac, can also be used in cooking. It is available fresh or frozen.

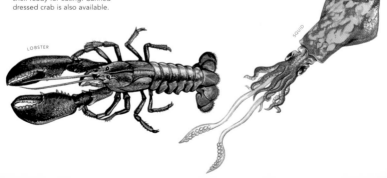

LOBSTER

SQUID

PREPARING FISH AND SHELLFISH

Regardless of the way you intend to cook fish, it must be cleaned first. This means removing the entrails and gills and sometimes the scales and fins. Your fish supplier will often do this for you. If not, use the following guidelines to approach the job step by step.

PREPARING FISH

Trimming round- and flatfish

If desired, using kitchen scissors, cut off the gills and fins if the fish is to be served whole. The head and tail may also be cut off using a sharp knife. Rinse the cavity under cold running water. Fins and scales obviously don't need to be removed if the fish is to be filleted or the skin is to be removed after cooking, or in the case of trout, as the scales are part of the skin.

Scaling roundfish

This is necessary for fish such as sea bass, salmon, and snapper.

Using the back of a knife or a fish scaler, scrape from the tail to the head, away from the direction of the scales, in short, firm strokes to remove the scales. As scales have a tendency to fly everywhere, you might find this a cleaner job if you put the fish in the sink, in a large plastic bag or cover it with a large dish towel. Rinse under cold running water and dry on paper towels.

PRESERVING FLAVOR

Cooking a whole fish with the skin on helps to give the fish flavor and prevent it from drying out during cooking.

Gutting flatfish

The entrails of a flatfish occupy only a small part of the fish's body cavity.

To remove them, open the cavity, which lies in the upper part of the body, under the gills, and clean out the entrails as for a roundfish.

Gutting roundfish

1 To remove the entrails, make a slit along the belly from the gills to the tail vent. Pull out the insides and clean away any blood in the cavity.

2 Remove the kidneys by running your thumbnail along the underside of the spine.

3 Rub with a little salt to remove the black skin.

Rinse under cold water and dry with paper towels.

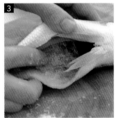

Pocket-cleaning roundfish

This is suitable for creating a pocket in a fish while keeping the body intact. The fish is cleaned through the gills, but it is not as simple a method as cleaning a roundfish along its belly.

1 Using a sharp knife, cut the end of the gut away from the anus, then open the gill covering and make a slit to reveal the throat.

2 With your fingers, pull out the guts through the throat cavity. Rinse under cold water, removing any remaining innards, and dry on paper towels.

Filleting flatfish

Four fillets, two from each side, are usually taken from a flatfish, although sometimes one large fillet is cut from each side and these are known as double or butterfly fillets. To make four fillets, put the fish on a cutting board with its tail toward you. Using a sharp knife, cut around the shape of the head and along the backbone from head to tail. With smooth cutting strokes, working from head to tail, separate the flesh from the bone. Turn the fish over and repeat on the other side.

Filleting large roundfish

Two fillets are taken from round fish, although very large round fish, such as porgy, can be filleted into four, following the flat fish method, or the whole sides can be lifted as described here and then each cut into two fillets.

Filleting small roundfish

This method, also known as butterfly boning, is suitable for small fish such as herrings, mackerel, and sardines that are usually cooked whole rather than in fillets.

1 Cut off the head and fins. Make a slit along the belly from the gills to the tail vent and remove the guts. Rinse under cold running water. Put the fish, skin-side up, on a cutting board, and with the heel of your hand, press firmly down on the backbone to loosen it.

1 Put the fish on its side on a cutting board, with its tail and backbone toward you. Make an angular cut around the gills to the top of the head. It is not necessary to remove either the head or the tail.

2 Cut along the backbone from the head to the tail in order to expose the backbone.

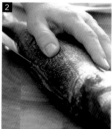

3 With smooth cutting strokes, working from head to tail, separate the flesh from the bones. Turn the flesh over and repeat on the other side, but this time working from tail to head.

2 Turn the fish over, cut the backbone near the head, then ease the backbone out with your fingers. Remove any pinbones as described in Pinboning Fish (see opposite), then cut off the tail.

Skinning whole roundfish

Whole roundfish are usually cooked with the skin on, which is then removed before serving.

1 With the tip of the knife, loosen the skin under the head. Then, with salted fingers, gently pull the skin down toward the tail, being careful not to break the flesh. Turn the fish over and repeat on the other side.

Skinning whole flatfish

Whole flatfish are usually cooked with the skin on. However, Dover and slip soles are traditionally skinned on the dark side only before cooking.

1 Using a sharp knife, make a small cut in the dark skin across the tail.

2 Should you wish to remove the skin before cooking, using a sharp knife, cut along the backbone and across the skin just below the head.

2 Slip your thumb between the skin and flesh of the fish and loosen the skin. Then, holding the tail end firmly with one hand and gripping the skin with a cloth or paper towels in the other hand, pull the skin upwards toward the head. A large pinch of salt may help you to grip the flesh.

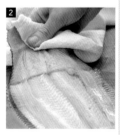

Pinboning fish

Small pinbones are to be found at the top of the flesh of roundfish fillets.

To remove them, feel for the bones with your fingertips and then remove them using a pair of tweezers.

Skinning fish fillets

Put the fish fillet, skin-side down, on a cutting board. Gripping the tail firmly in one hand with a cloth or paper towels and with a knife held at an angle, remove the flesh by making a gentle sawing action away from you. A large pinch of salt may help you to grip the tail.

Preparing a fish noisette from a fish steak

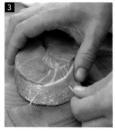

1 After removing the pinbones, using a sharp knife, remove the skin from the flesh halfway around the steak.

2 Curl the skinned piece of fish into the center and wrap the rest of the steak around the outside.

3 Wrap the loose piece of skin around the steak and secure the whole noisette with wooden toothpicks.

Boning a Dover or slip sole

Dover and slip soles can be boned in preparation for stuffing. To do this, skin both sides of the fish as described under Skinning Whole Flatfish (see page 31).

1 Put the fish on a cutting board with its tail toward you and, using a sharp knife, cut around the shape of the head and along the backbone from head to tail.

2 With smooth cutting strokes, working from head to tail, lift the flesh from the bone, stopping when you reach the fins. Leave the fillet completely attached to the head and tail. Turn the fish around and separate the fillet on the other side of the fish in the same way.

3 Turn the fish over and repeat on the other side, leaving the fillets attached to the fins, head, and tail in the same way. Using kitchen scissors, cut away all around the backbone and remove it.

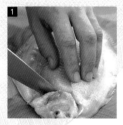

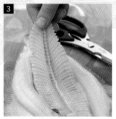

PREPARING CEPHALOPODS

Squid

Put the squid on a cutting board and, grasping the body in one hand, gently pull off the head and tentacles with the other hand. The body entrails will come away at the same time and should be discarded.

1 Cut off the edible tentacles just in front of the eyes and reserve, then squeeze out the small, hard beak and discard.

2 Remove the transparent quill that runs along the length of the body of the squid.

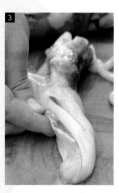

3 Carefully remove one or two of the ink sacs from the head so that you do not pierce them and set them aside if you want to use the ink in another recipe. Discard the head.

4 Rub off the thin, dark, outer membrane with your fingers. Rinse under cold running water and dry on paper towels.

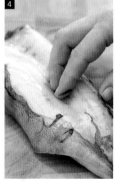

SQUID INK

Squid ink can be used in a black risotto. To use, put the sac in a cup and pierce with the tip of a sharp knife. Dilute the ink with a little water, then pass through a strainer.

Octopus

Put the octopus on a cutting board and, grasping the body in one hand, firmly pull off the head and tentacles with the other hand. The body entrails will come away at the same time and should be discarded along with the ink sac. Cut off the edible tentacles just in front of the eyes. Rinse the body and tentacles under cold running water and dry on paper towels, then beat well with a rolling pin or wooden meat mallet to tenderize the flesh.

PREPARING SHELLFISH

Crab

Crabs are usually sold cooked, but should you buy a live one, the most humane and least traumatic way of killing it is by the following method. Put the live crab in a plastic bag in the freezer for 2 hours to put it to sleep. Bring a large pan of heavily salted water to a boil, adding 1/3 cup salt to every 4 cups. Remove the crab from the freezer, immediately plunge the unconscious crab into the water, and cover the pan. Return to a boil and let simmer for 15 minutes, allowing an extra 10 minutes for each additional crab. Let cool in the water.

To prepare a cooked crab, have 2 bowls ready, one for white meat and one for brown meat. Put the crab on its back on a cutting board. Gripping a claw firmly in one hand and as close to the body as possible, twist it off. Remove the other claw and the legs in the same way.

1 Break the claws in half by bending them backward at the joint. Crack the shells of the claws and larger legs with a rolling pin and remove the white meat with a skewer or teaspoon handle. Set aside the small legs for garnishing.

Put the crab on its back with its eyes and mouth facing away from you.

2 Remove the stomach sac and mouth, which are attached to the back shell, and discard them.

3 Gripping the shell firmly, press the body section upward and gently pull them apart. Remove the soft gray gills that are attached along the edges of the body and discard.

4 Cut the body into two or four pieces and carefully pick out the flesh. Scoop out the brown meat from the shell.

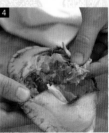

Lobster

A live lobster should be cooked in the same way as a crab (see opposite), but when you remove it from the freezer, weigh it quickly before plunging it into the water. Calculate the cooking time by allowing 18 minutes for the first 1 lb 2 oz/500 g and an extra 11 minutes for every additional 1 lb 2 oz/500 g.

1 To prepare a cooked lobster, put it on a cutting board and twist off the claws and pincers. Crack open the large claws and remove the flesh from them, discarding the membrane. The small claws can be reserved for garnishing.

2 Using the tip of a sharp knife, split the shell of the lobster in half from head to tail.

3 Remove the flesh from the tail, reserving the coral (only found in females and at certain times of the year) and, using a skewer, scrape out the flesh from the back legs.

4 Remove and discard the threadlike intestine, the stomach sac, and the spongy gills from the lobster.

DON'T SOAK OR FEED

Never soak shellfish, particularly filter feeders such as oysters, mussels, and clams, in cold water as this will kill them. They should also not be fed, for example with oatmeal, while storing them in the refrigerator, as this can also leave them gaping open and dead.

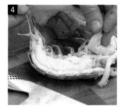

Shrimp

1 To peel a shrimp, hold its head between your thumb and index finger and, using the fingers of your other hand, hold the tail and gently pinch and pull off the tail shell.

2 Holding the body, pull off the head, body shell, and claws.

3 To devein a shrimp, using the tip of a sharp knife or skewer, carefully pull out the dark vein that runs down the shrimp's back and discard.

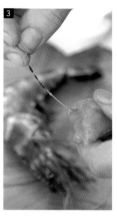

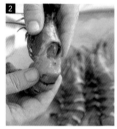

Oyster

Scrub each oyster shell with a stiff scrubbing brush under cold running water to clean. To open an oyster (known as to shuck an oyster), put it on a cutting board, with the rounded side down, and cover with a clean dish towel to protect your hands.

1 Holding the oyster in the cloth and using a strong, short knife or, ideally, a shucking knife, insert the knife at the hinge and prise the shell upward to open the oyster shell. Take great care when doing this.

2 Slide the knife along the inside of the upper shell to cut the muscle and release the oyster. Try to reserve as much of the juice as possible. Oysters served raw "on the half shell" are served with their juices in the bottom shell.

Clam

Scrub each clam with a stiff scrubbing brush under cold running water to clean the shell, then put on a cutting board or hold each clam in a cloth in the palm of your hand and prise the shell open at the hinge with a knife, ideally a clam knife.

If the clams are very difficult to open, they can be helped by putting them on a baking sheet in a very hot oven for 4–5 minutes until they begin to open.

Loosen the clams and leave each one in half of the shell if you are intending to serve them raw. Set aside any juice from the clams, as this can be strained and used in a sauce. It should certainly not be discarded.

Mussel

Clean each mussel by scrubbing or scraping the shell under cold running water to remove any barnacles, mud, or seaweed.

Pull away any beards that are attached to the mussel shells. It is the the beard that the mussel uses to cling to the rocks so you will need to tug hard. If the mussel is open and will not close when tapped sharply with the back of a knife, it is dead and should be discarded.

Also discard any with broken shells or any that feel particularly heavy, as these are probably filled with sand. Put the mussels in a colander and rinse well under cold running water, then drain well.

Scallop

1 Scrub each scallop shell with a stiff scrubbing brush under cold running water to remove as much sand as possible.

2 Discard any scallops that are open and will not close when tapped sharply with the back of a knife. Using a strong knife, prise the shell open. If the scallops are very difficult to open, they can be helped by putting them on a baking tray, with their rounded side uppermost, in a very hot oven for 4–5 minutes until the shells begin to open.

3 Remove and discard the gray beard that surrounds each scallop and the black thread and stomach bag. Detach the scallop and coral from the shell with a spoon. Rinse under cold running water and dry on paper towels.

COOKING FISH AND SHELLFISH

Fish lends itself to most cooking methods, as described over the following pages, and the methods can be applied in the same way regardless of the fish. When fish is cooked, it should look opaque, right through to the bone, and the flakes of the fish should be more obvious. Try to avoid overcooking, as it will make the fish shrink, toughen, and become dry.

DEEP-FRYING

Small whole fish and small pieces of fish and shellfish, coated in a barrier such as flour, batter, or egg and bread crumbs, are suitable for this cooking method. It is this protective coating that keeps the fish moist, gives it crispness, and seals in the flavor. Here are a few rules:

• Use a deep-fat fryer, a heavy-bottom pan, or a wok large enough so that the fish is completely immersed in the oil.

• Don't fill the pan more than half full.

• Use a vegetable oil, such as sunflower-seed or corn oil, but not olive oil as it spits.

• The temperature of the oil should be between 350–375°F/180–190°C so that the coating is sealed immediately, which protects the fish from the hot fat and prevents the fat from soaking in and the food becoming greasy. A simple way to test to see if the temperature is correct is to drop a cube of bread in the oil. If it rises to the surface, fizzes immediately, and turns brown in 30 seconds, the oil is hot enough.

• Cook the fish in batches so that the pan is not overcrowded and the temperature of the oil doesn't drop. This will assure that the fish is thoroughly cooked, evenly browned, and crisp.

• Oil that has been used for deep-frying can be used two or three times before being discarded.

KEEP IT WHITE

Lemon juice, white wine, or
vinegar, added to the liquid
when poaching or steaming
fish, helps to keep the flesh
of the fish white and firm.

PAN-FRYING

This is suitable for whole fish,
steaks, fillets, and shellfish, which
are sometimes coated in flour
before pan-frying to protect their
flesh, making them crispy, and
sealing in the flavor. Use a large,
uncovered skillet so that the fish
will fit comfortably in it as, if it is
overpacked, the temperature of
the fat will drop. It is important
to use the minimum amount of
fat and to keep it hot so that the
fish browns without absorbing
the fat and becoming greasy.
The fat used can be a vegetable
oil, such as sunflower-seed oil,
clarified butter, or butter, which
gives a good flavor. If you are
solely using butter, heat until it
is foaming, but watch it carefully
as it burns quickly. Adding a little
oil to it helps, as the oil reaches a
high temperature before the
butter burns.

Don't turn or move the fish too
often, as it will stick to the
bottom of the pan. Allow it to
brown first before turning. If
cooking thick pieces of fish, pan-
fry quickly until browned, then
reduce the heat and cook until
the flesh is tender.

STIR-FRYING

This is suitable for small pieces of
firm-textured fish that need only
the quickest of cooking. A wok is
traditionally used, as its sloping
sides make it perfect for
continually stirring and tossing
the fish. However, a large skillet
can be used as a substitute. Only
a small amount of oil is needed
and this should be heated until
very hot before adding the fish.

POACHING

This is a moist method of cooking
most fish, immersed in a liquid,
on the stove or in the oven. A
fish poacher or large pan is used
on the stove or a large roasting
pan, covered with foil, in the
oven. The poaching liquid can be
Court Bouillon (see page 44),
Fish Stock (see page 44), wine,
cider, beer, milk, or flavored
water, and sometimes this liquid
is then made into a sauce to
serve with the fish. It is important
that the liquid never boils but
just trembles, so that the fish
doesn't fall apart.

To poach fish, first weigh the
fish. Heat the liquid in the pan,
add the fish, cover, and let
simmer very gently, allowing
10–15 minutes per 1 lb/450 g,
according to the thickness of the
fish, or about 20 minutes for a
small piece of fish.

STEAMING

This is a gentle, moist method of cooking whole fish, fillets, steaks, and shellfish in a water vapor over boiling water. A steamer, with a tight-fitting lid to trap the steam, is needed but if not available, you can improvise by cooking the fish between two greased plates over a pan of boiling water. You could even use a pan with a tight-fitting lid and a strainer. The fish should be well seasoned otherwise it may taste bland. The water in the pan should be boiling, but watch that it does not bubble up over the fish during cooking.

SEARING AND GRIDDLING

Searing and griddling are suitable for cooking whole and thicker pieces of fish and produce browned skin and flesh. The methods are the same except that seared fish is cooked in a heavy-bottom skillet and griddled fish is cooked on a cast-iron, ridged stovetop grill pan or flat griddle plate. The grill pan or griddle plate is first wiped with just a little vegetable oil, heated until it is very, very hot, and the fish, which should also be brushed with a little oil, is placed on it and cooked on both sides until browned.

BROILING AND BARBECUING

Whole fish, steaks, fillets, and skewered pieces of fish all lend themselves to these dry cooking methods, but for good results, their thickness should be no more than 2 inches/5 cm and whole fish should be scored at the thickest part of the flesh so that the heat penetrates and cooks the fish right through. Oily fish are particularly suitable, as the natural oils baste the flesh during cooking. Broiled and barbecued fish also benefit from being marinated before cooking and the marinade should be basted over the fish while it is cooking to keep it moist.

It is very important to preheat the broiler at its highest temperature before cooking, as intense heat, and being cooked as close to the heat source as possible, is the secret of successful broiled fish. This will cook the fish so that it is browned and crisp on the outside and moist inside. Barbecues should also be preheated and the flames and smoke allowed to die down so that the fish is only cooked over the red hot embers. Brush the broiler rack or foil, if using to line the rack, barbecue rack, or a fish barbecue holder, and also the fish, with vegetable oil to prevent the fish from sticking. As barbecuing is a method of cooking by intense heat, the fish can dry out quickly, so you may prefer to wrap it in oiled foil, which will help to keep it moist.

BAKING

Baking is an ideal method of cooking whole fish, particularly stuffed fish, as well as steaks and fillets. As this is a method of cooking by dry heat, a tablespoon of butter and a little stock, milk, lemon juice, or wine is added to the fish and the fish should be covered to prevent it from drying. This can be done either by covering the dish with foil or by wrapping the entire fish in waxed paper, known as en papillote (see the recipe for Porgy en Papillote on page 208). When cooked en papillote, the fish is served in its paper bag.

BRAISING

This is a moist, one-pot method of cooking, usually a whole fish, on the stove or in the oven. The fish is placed on a bed of vegetables with just enough liquid to cover the vegetables, and the pan or dish should always be covered. The fish is then cooked gently. At the end of cooking, the vegetables are discarded and the liquid is usually used to make a sauce to serve with the fish.

STEWING

Whole fish, chunks of fish, and shellfish can be cooked in liquid with other ingredients, such as vegetables and flavorings, to form a stew. The fish flavors the liquid but, unlike a meat stew where it is cooked for a long time, the fish in a fish stew is often added to the liquid toward the end of cooking so that it is not overcooked.

Classic fish stews include Bouillabaisse (see page 121), which is traditionally served as two courses, Bourride, where the fish is not left whole as in Bouillabaisse, Matelote, made with freshwater fish, and Cioppino (see page 122) made from shellfish.

MICROWAVING

Microwave ovens are excellent for cooking fish because, as the fish cooks in its own juices, it is a moist form of cooking. However, a few rules should be observed for successful results.

• Arrange the thickest part of the fish toward the edge of the dish.
• Tuck in the tail end of fillets to create a more even shape.
• Don't overseason fish as this causes a rapid loss of moisture.
• Cut pieces of fish into the same size and thickness so that they cook evenly.
• Slash the skin of whole fish in two or three places to allow steam to escape and prevent it from spitting during cooking.
• Cover fish during cooking, unless the recipe says otherwise, to retain the moisture.
• Don't fry fish in the microwave.

DON'T FIDDLE

When searing, griddling, broiling, and barbecuing, don't be tempted to turn or move the fish around while cooking, as it may stick to the pan, griddle, or rack and fall apart. Ideally, turn the fish only once during cooking.

PREPARING SUSHI

Sushi originated centuries ago as a way of extending the shelf life of dried fish by placing it between layers of vinegared rice. The word sushi refers to the vinegared rice, but the term has been extended to describe a finger-size piece of raw fish or seafood on a bed of cold vinegared rice.

EQUIPMENT NEEDED

Very little specialized equipment is required, although you can buy sushi-making kits in various outlets, including larger supermarkets. The key to the technique is a bamboo sushi mat with which to make the most common form, rolled sushi. A kit may include a special mixing tub, a pressing box, and a spatula.

WHICH FISH?

Meatier types of roundfish, such as cod, tuna, salmon, trout, mackerel, and eel, are all suitable for sushi, as are shrimp, lobster, squid, scallops, crab, and fish roe. Smoked versions of haddock, salmon, trout, and mackerel are also popular. Many sushi recipes use raw fish. Always buy it from a reliable supplier who offers "sushi" or "sashimi grade" fish, which is as fresh as possible, because raw fish contains more bacteria and parasites than cooked fish. Similarly, look for shellfish that come from certified waters. Only buy fish or shellfish on the day you intend to eat it and keep it refrigerated.

PREPARING SUSHI RICE

Sushi is a short-grained rice, and several brands are available. The hot, cooked rice is tipped into a large, shallow dish and sushi rice seasoning spread over the surface. With one hand you mix in the seasoning with a spatula; with the other you fan the rice to cool it quickly. The finished rice should have a shiny appearance and be at room temperature.

PRESENTING SUSHI

Presentation is all, and the best sushi are minor works of culinary art. You need all the ingredients assembled, the rice cooled and sauces prepared so that you can serve the sushi immediately.

Scattered sushi

This is where sushi rice is mixed loosely with other ingredients, and is very easy to make. It is often served as an attractive, individual bowl for each person.

Rolled sushi

These are best made using a sushi mat.

A sheet of nori (dried seaweed), is placed on the bamboo mat and the filling heaped along the bottom third of the nori.

By folding the mat over the filling, then lifting the mat and keeping an even pressure along the length, the roll is formed.

It is cut using a very sharp, wet knife into circles, which are then turned on one end to present the filling.

Boat sushi

These dishes are prepared by wrapping nori around rice molded into oval shapes. Using nori is an ideal way to serve sushi with fish roe or soft toppings that would otherwise be messy to handle.

Pressed sushi

This type is made by pressing the rice into a three-piece bamboo box, although you can improvise using a loose-bottom pan or terrine pan with drop-down sides. If you have a fixed-bottom pan, the sushi has to be made upside down, and the sushi turned out, after the flavors have had time to mix and develop.

BASIC RECIPES

The recipes in this book provide an unlimited variety of delicious fish meals. Some of the recipes

use a common basic recipe which are referred to on these pages, or you can use these basic

recipes as an addition to a dish of your choice.

FISH STOCK

MAKES ABOUT 6 CUPS

2–3 lb/900 g–1.3 kg fish heads, bones, and tails, with any
  large bones cracked and without any gills
5 cups water
generous 2 cups dry white wine
1 onion, thinly sliced
1 leek, halved, rinsed and chopped
1 carrot, peeled and sliced
6 fresh flat-leaf parsley sprigs
1 bay leaf
4 black peppercorns, lightly crushed

Put the fish trimmings, water, and wine in a large heavy-
bottom pan over medium-high heat and slowly bring to
a boil, skimming the surface constantly to remove the
gray foam.

When the foam stops forming, reduce the heat to low,
add the remaining ingredients, and let the stock
simmer for 30 minutes, skimming the surface
occasionally if necessary.

Strain the stock and discard the flavoring ingredients.
The stock is now ready to use or can be left to cool
completely, then chilled for 1 day, as long as it is
brought to a full rolling boil before use.
Alternatively, it can be frozen
for up to 6 months.

COURT BOUILLON

MAKES ABOUT 2 1/2 CUPS

3 1/2 cups cold water
3 1/2 cups dry white wine
3 tbsp white wine vinegar
2 large carrots, coarsely chopped
1 onion, coarsely chopped
2 celery stalks, coarsely chopped
2 leeks, coarsely chopped
2 garlic cloves, coarsely chopped
2 fresh bay leaves
4 parsley sprigs
6 black peppercorns
1 tsp salt

Put all the ingredients into a large pan and slowly bring
to a boil. Cover and let simmer gently for 30 minutes.

Strain the liquid through a fine strainer into a clean pan.
Bring to a boil again and let simmer fast, uncovered for
15–20 minutes, until reduced to 2½ cups.

Simmer the fish in the court bouillon, according to the
length of time required to cook. Drain the fish.

BÉCHAMEL SAUCE

1¼ cups milk
4 cloves
1 bay leaf
pinch of freshly grated
  nutmeg
2 tbsp butter or margarine
2 tbsp all-purpose flour
salt and pepper

Put the milk in a pan and add the cloves, bay leaf, and nutmeg. Gradually bring to a boil. Remove from the heat and leave for 15 minutes.

Melt the butter in another pan and stir in the flour to make a roux. Cook gently, stirring, for 1 minute. Remove the pan from the heat.

Strain the milk and gradually blend into the roux. Return the pan to the heat and gently bring to a boil, stirring, until the sauce thickens. Season to taste.

VARIATIONS

All sorts of ingredients can be added to the basic Béchamel recipe to make interesting sauces that go particularly well with vegetables and fish.

Watercress Sauce
Add 1 small bunch of watercress, finely chopped, to the basic sauce.

Parsley Sauce
Add 2 tablespoons finely chopped fresh parsley to the basic sauce.

Mushroom Sauce
Wash and finely slice 4 oz/115 g white mushrooms, and add them to the basic sauce with 1 tablespoon of finely chopped fresh tarragon.

Lemon Sauce
Add some finely grated lemon rind and juice to the basic sauce.

Mustard Sauce
Add 1 tablespoon French mustard and a squeeze of lemon juice to the basic sauce.

HOLLANDAISE SAUCE

2 tbsp white wine vinegar
2 tbsp water
6 black peppercorns
3 egg yolks
1⅛ cups unsalted butter
2 tsp lemon juice
salt and pepper

Put the wine vinegar and water into a small pan with the peppercorns, bring to a boil, then reduce the heat and let simmer until it is reduced to 1 tablespoon (take care, this happens very quickly). Strain.

Mix the egg yolks in a blender or food processor and add the strained vinegar while the machine is running.

Melt the butter in a small pan and heat until it turns almost brown. Again, while the blender is running, add three-quarters of the butter, the lemon juice, then the remaining butter, and season well with salt and pepper.

Turn the sauce into a serving bowl or keep warm for up to 1 hour in a bowl over a pan of warm water. If serving cold, let cool, and store in the refrigerator for up to 2 days.

MAYONNAISE

2 egg yolks
pinch of salt, plus extra for seasoning
²/₃ cup sunflower-seed oil
²/₃ cup olive oil
1 tbsp white wine vinegar
2 tsp Dijon mustard
pepper

Beat the egg yolks with a pinch of salt. Combine the oils in a pitcher. Gradually add one quarter of the oil mixture to the beaten egg, a drop at a time, beating constantly with a whisk or electric mixer.

Beat in the vinegar, then continue adding the oils in a steady stream, beating constantly.

Stir in the mustard and season to taste with salt and pepper.

GREEK GARLIC SAUCE

³/₄ cup whole blanched almonds
3 tbsp fresh white bread crumbs
2 large garlic cloves, crushed
2 tsp lemon juice
salt and pepper
²/₃ cup extra virgin olive oil
4 tbsp hot water

Put the almonds in a food processor and blend until finely ground. Add the bread crumbs, garlic, lemon juice, salt and pepper and mix well together.

With the machine running, very slowly pour in the oil to form a smooth, thick mixture. When all the oil has been added, blend in the water.

Turn the mixture into a bowl and let chill in the refrigerator for at least 2 hours before serving.

TARTARE SAUCE

2 large egg yolks
2 tsp Dijon mustard
³/₄ tsp salt, or to taste
white pepper
2 tbsp lemon juice or white wine vinegar
about 1¹/₄ cups sunflower-seed oil
10 gherkins, finely chopped
1 tbsp capers, finely chopped
1 tbsp flat-leaf parsley, finely chopped

Blend the egg yolks with the mustard, salt, and white pepper to taste in a food processor, blender, or by hand. Add the lemon juice and blend again.

With the motor still running or still beating, add the oil, drop by drop at first. When the sauce begins to thicken, the oil can then be added in a slow, steady stream.

Stir in the gherkins, capers, and parsley. Taste and adjust the seasoning with extra salt, pepper, and lemon juice if necessary. If the sauce seems too thick, slowly add 1 tablespoon of hot water, light cream, or lemon juice.

Use at once or store in an airtight container in the refrigerator for up to 1 week.

AIOLI

1 large egg yolk
1 tbsp white wine vinegar or lemon juice
2 large garlic cloves, peeled
salt and pepper
5 tbsp extra virgin olive oil
5 tbsp sunflower-seed oil

Put the egg yolk, vinegar, garlic, and salt and pepper to taste in a bowl and whisk until all the ingredients are well blended.

Add the olive oil, then the sunflower-seed oil, drop by drop at first, and then, when it begins to thicken, in a slow, steady stream until the sauce is thick and smooth.

SUSHI RICE

scant 1¼ cups sushi rice
generous 1¼ cups water
1 piece of kombu
2 tbsp sushi rice seasoning

Wash the sushi rice under cold running water until the water running through it is clear, then drain the rice. Put the rice in a pan with the water and the kombu, then cover and bring to a boil as quickly as you can.

Remove the kombu, then turn the heat down and let simmer for 10 minutes. Turn off the heat and let the rice stand for 15 minutes. Do not at any point take the lid off the pan once you have removed the kombu.

Put the hot rice in a large, very shallow bowl and pour the sushi rice seasoning evenly over the surface of the rice. Use one hand to mix the seasoning carefully into the rice with quick cutting strokes using a spatula, and the other to fan the sushi rice in order to cool it quickly.

The sushi rice should look shiny and be at room temperature when you are ready to use it.

BEURRE BLANC

3 tbsp very finely chopped shallots
2 bay leaves
6 black peppercorns, lightly crushed
3 tbsp white wine, such as Muscadet
3 tbsp white wine vinegar
1½ tbsp heavy cream
¾ cup unsalted butter, cut into small pieces
2 tsp chopped fresh tarragon
salt and pepper

Put the shallots, bay leaves, peppercorns, wine, and vinegar in a small pan over medium–high heat and boil until reduced to about 1 tablespoon. Strain the mixture through a nonmetallic strainer, then return the liquid to the pan.

Stir the cream into the liquid and bring to a boil, then reduce the heat to low. Whisk in the butter, piece by piece, not adding the next until the previous one is melted. Whisking constantly and lifting the pan off the heat occasionally will help prevent the sauce from separating. Stir in the tarragon and salt and pepper to taste.

Fish and shellfish make ideal finger food—tantalizing, luxurious, melt-in-the-mouth morsels that have instant eye and taste bud appeal. Whether you are catering for an informal get-together or for special-occasion entertaining, these recipes for both hot and cold nibbles are easy to prepare yet impressive in effect.

FISH NIBBLES

Homemade sushi will certainly provide the wow factor, and here are some stylish blocks, bars, and rolls that can all be prepared in advance. Shrimp come perfectly proportioned for popping in the mouth, so we have them sizzling in aromatic oil or wrapped in ham. But who can resist a crisp, pastry package hot from the oven? The choice is yours, from crab-filled won tons and phyllo packages to tuna boreks.

serves 6 | *prep* 15 minutes, plus 1 hour chilling | *cook* no cooking required

TARAMASALATA

8 oz/225 g smoked cod roe or fresh
  gray mullet roe
1 small onion, quartered
1 cup fresh white bread crumbs
1 large garlic clove, crushed
grated rind and juice of 1 large lemon
²/₃ cup extra virgin olive oil
6 tbsp hot water
pepper
crackers, potato chips, or pita bread,
  to serve

TO GARNISH
pitted black Greek olives, sliced
capers, rinsed

Remove the skin from the roe. Put the onion in a food processor and process to chop finely. Add the roe in small pieces and process until smooth. Add the bread crumbs, garlic, and lemon rind and juice and mix well together.

With the motor running, very slowly pour in the oil through the feed tube, then blend in the water. Season to taste with pepper.

Turn the mixture into a serving bowl, then cover and let chill in the refrigerator for at least 1 hour before serving. Serve garnished with olives and capers and accompany with crackers, potato chips, or pita bread.

makes 18 | *prep* 30 minutes | *cook* 15–30 minutes

TUNA & TOMATO BOREKS

about 18 sheets phyllo pastry,
  15 x 6 inches/38 x 15 cm each,
  thawed if frozen
vegetable oil, for sealing and
  pan-frying
sea salt, to garnish
lemon wedges, to serve

FILLING
2 hard-cooked eggs, shelled and
  finely chopped
7 oz/200 g canned tuna in brine,
  drained
1 tbsp chopped fresh dill
1 tomato, peeled, seeded, and very
  finely chopped
¼ tsp cayenne pepper
salt and pepper

To make the filling, put the eggs in a bowl with the tuna and dill and mash the mixture until blended.

Stir in the tomato, taking care not to break it up too much. Season with the cayenne pepper and salt and pepper to taste. Set aside.

Lay a sheet of phyllo pastry out on a counter with a short side nearest to you, keeping the remaining sheets covered with a damp dish towel. Arrange about 1 tablespoon of the filling in a line along the short side, about ½ inch/1 cm in from the end and 1 inch/2.5 cm in from both long sides.

Make one tight roll to enclose the filling, then fold in both long sides for the length of the phyllo. Continue rolling up to the end. Use a little vegetable oil to seal the end. Repeat to make 17 more rolls, or until all the filling has been used up.

Heat 1 inch/2.5 cm of oil in a skillet to 350–375°F/180–190°C, or until a cube of bread browns in 30 seconds. Deep-fry 2–3 boreks at a time for 2–3 minutes until golden brown. Remove with a slotted spoon and drain well on paper towels. Sprinkle with sea salt. Serve hot or at room temperature with lemon wedges for squeezing over.

makes 12 | prep 30 minutes | cook 4–6 minutes

TUNA SESAME BLOCKS

3¼ x 2½-inch/8 x 6-cm piece
   center-cut tuna fillet,
   ¾ inch/2 cm thick
2 tsp sesame oil
2 tbsp toasted sesame seeds
3 small sheets nori, cut lengthwise
   into 4 strips
2 tbsp vegetable oil

Cut the tuna into 12 cubes. Put the sesame oil in a shallow bowl or on a plate and the sesame seeds in a separate bowl or on a plate. Roll the tuna cubes in the sesame oil, followed by the sesame seeds.

Lay the nori strips out on a counter. Roll each tuna cube in a sheet of nori, trimming off any excess so that the nori goes round the tuna once with only a little overlap. Moisten the top edge of the nori with a little water to seal the end.

Heat the vegetable oil in a large skillet over high heat and add the tuna cubes, standing them up on one nori-free end. Cook for 2 minutes, then turn over to cook the other nori-free end. The sesame seeds should be a dark brown, but not burned, and the tuna should have cooked most of the way through, leaving a rare patch in the center. If you prefer your tuna completely cooked, cook each end for a little longer. Serve hot or warm.

makes 24 | prep 20 minutes | cook 8 minutes

SEVEN-SPICED SALMON ROLLS

1 salmon fillet, about 5½ oz/150 g
sichimi togarashi (seven-spice
  powder)
dried red pepper flakes, for sprinkling
1 tbsp vegetable oil
1 quantity freshly cooked Sushi Rice
6 small sheets toasted nori
2 tbsp Japanese mayonnaise

TO SERVE
shoyu (Japanese soy sauce)
wasabi paste
pickled ginger

Remove and discard the skin and bones from the salmon fillet. Dust the surface heavily with sichimi togarashi and sprinkle over a few red pepper flakes. Heat the oil in a skillet over medium heat, add the salmon, and cook on both sides for 8 minutes, or until cooked through. Let cool, then flake into large pieces.

Divide the rice into 6 equal portions. Lay a sheet of nori out shiny-side down on a rolling mat with the longest end toward you and, using wet hands, spread 1 portion of the rice in an even layer on the nori, leaving ¾ inch/2 cm of nori visible at the end farthest away from you. Don't squash the rice or make the layer too thick—you should be able to see the nori through the rice.

Spread the mayonnaise onto the rice at the end nearest to you. Lay one-sixth of the salmon on top of the mayonnaise.

To roll the sushi, fold the mat over, starting at the end where the ingredients are and tucking in the end of the nori to start the roll. Keep rolling, lifting up the mat as you go, and keeping the pressure even but gentle until you have finished the roll. Moisten the top edge of the nori with a little water to seal the end.

Remove the roll from the mat and cut it into 4 even-size pieces with a very sharp, wet knife. Turn the pieces on end and arrange them on a plate. Repeat with the remaining ingredients. Serve with shoyu, wasabi, and pickled ginger.

makes 8–10 | *prep* 15 minutes, plus 15 minutes' chilling | *cook* no cooking required

PRESSED SUSHI BARS WITH SMOKED SALMON & CUCUMBER

vegetable oil, for oiling
1/2 quantity freshly cooked Sushi Rice
2 tbsp Japanese mayonnaise
7 oz/200 g smoked salmon
1/2 cucumber, peeled and cut into very
   thin slices

TO GARNISH
lemon wedges
handful of fresh mint sprigs

Oil an *oshi waku* or terrine pan (preferably with drop-down sides) and line it with a piece of plastic wrap so that the plastic wrap hangs over the edges. This is to help you lift the sushi out later. Pack the pan 1¼ inches/3 cm full with the rice. Spread a layer of mayonnaise on top of the rice. Arrange the smoked salmon and cucumber in diagonal strips on top of the rice, doubling up the smoked salmon layers if you have enough so that the topping is quite thick. Cover the top of the rice with a strip of plastic wrap, put another terrine pan on top, and weight down with a couple of food cans.

Chill the sushi in the refrigerator for 15 minutes. Remove the cans and the top pan, then lift out the sushi. Cut the sushi in 8–10 pieces with a very sharp, wet knife. Garnish with lemon wedges and mint sprigs before serving.

serves 4 | prep 10 minutes | cook 1 minute

SCATTERED SUSHI
WITH SMOKED MACKEREL

8 snow peas
2-inch/5-cm piece daikon
1 quantity freshly cooked Sushi Rice
juice and finely grated rind of 1 lemon
2 scallions, finely chopped
2 smoked mackerel fillets, skinned,
    cut into diagonal strips
1/2 cucumber, peeled and cut
    into slices

TO GARNISH
pickled ginger
strips of toasted nori
wasabi paste

Bring a pan of lightly salted water to a boil, add the snow peas, and blanch for 1 minute. Drain and set aside to cool. Shred the daikon using the finest setting on a mandolin or a very sharp knife. If you are using a knife, cut the daikon into long, thin slices and cut each slice along its length as finely as you can.

Mix the rice with the lemon juice and rind.

Divide the rice between 4 wooden or ceramic bowls—they should be about 3/4 inch/2 cm full. Sprinkle the scallions over the top. Arrange the mackerel, cucumber, snow peas, and daikon on top of the rice. Garnish with pickled ginger, nori strips, and a small mound of wasabi.

serves 4 | prep 15 minutes | cook 15–30 minutes

SEAFOOD TEMPURA

8 large raw shrimp, shelled and
   deveined
8 squid rings
5¹/₂ oz/150 g package tempura mix
4 live scallops, shucked and cleaned
7 oz/200 g firm white fish fillets, cut
   into strips
vegetable oil, for deep-frying
few drops sesame oil
shoyu (Japanese soy sauce), to serve

Make little cuts on the underside of the
shrimp to keep them straight while they
cook. Remove and discard any membranes
from the squid rings.

Combine the tempura mix with the amount
of water specified on the package instructions
in a large bowl until you have a lumpy batter
full of air bubbles. Do not try to make the
batter smooth or it will be heavy, and use it
straight away or it will settle.

Drop all the seafood into the batter.

Heat the vegetable oil in a deep-fat fryer,
large, heavy-bottom pan, or wok to
350–375°F/180–190°C, or until a cube of bread
browns in 30 seconds. Add the sesame oil.

Deep-fry 2–3 tempura pieces at a time for
2–3 minutes until a very light golden color
(if you deep-fry too many pieces at one time,
the oil temperature will drop and the batter
will be soggy). Remove with a slotted spoon
and drain off as much oil as possible, then
drain on paper towels for 30 seconds.

Serve this dish very hot with shoyu as a
dipping sauce.

serves 4 | prep 15 minutes | cook 20–25 minutes

FISH FRITTERS

To make the batter, put the flour and salt in a large bowl. Make a well in the center and pour in the egg and olive oil. Gradually add the water, beating constantly and drawing the flour from the side into the liquid, to form a smooth batter.

Remove and discard any skin and bones from the fish fillets and cut the flesh into 2-inch/5-cm chunks. Lightly dust with flour.

generous ³/₄ cup all-purpose flour,
  plus extra for dusting
pinch of salt
1 egg, beaten
1 tbsp olive oil
²/₃ cup warm water
1 lb 8 oz/675 g white fish fillets, such
  as well-soaked salt cod, angler fish
  or cod
sunflower-seed oil, for deep-frying
lemon wedges, to garnish

TO SERVE
aïoli
radishes

Heat the sunflower-seed oil in a deep-fat fryer, large, heavy-bottom pan, or wok to 350–375°F/180–190°C, or until a cube of bread browns in 30 seconds. Dip each fish piece into the batter to coat and deep-fry in small batches for 5 minutes, or until crisp and golden (if you deep-fry too many pieces at one time, the oil temperature will drop and the batter will be soggy). Remove with a slotted spoon and drain on paper towels.

Serve the fish fritters hot, garnished with lemon wedges, and accompanied by aïoli and a bowl of radishes.

serves 4 | *prep* 10 minutes | *cook* 20 minutes

BAGNA CAUDA

6 tbsp olive oil
6 tbsp butter
4 garlic cloves, chopped
3¹/₂ oz/100 g canned anchovy fillets
  in oil, drained and chopped
6 tbsp light cream

TO SERVE
blanched asparagus spears
blanched broccoli florets
strips of red bell pepper
strips of pita bread

Heat the oil in a fondue pot over low heat, add the butter, and stir until melted. Add the garlic and cook, stirring constantly, for 4 minutes.

Add the anchovies and cook, stirring frequently, for 12–15 minutes, then stir in the cream. Keep the dip warm in the fondue pot over very low heat while you pass round a selection of asparagus, broccoli, red bell pepper, and pita bread strips for dipping.

makes 32 | prep 15 minutes | cook 10–15 minutes

DEVILS & ANGELS ON HORSEBACK

DEVILS
8 rindless Canadian bacon slices
8 canned anchovy fillets in oil, drained
16 whole blanched almonds
16 ready-to-eat prunes

ANGELS
8 rindless Canadian bacon slices
16 smoked oysters, drained if canned

Preheat the oven to 400°F/200°C. For the devils, cut each bacon slice lengthwise in half and gently stretch with the back of a knife. Cut each anchovy fillet lengthwise in half. Wrap an anchovy half around each almond and press them into the cavity where the pits have been removed from the prunes. Wrap a strip of bacon around each prune and secure with a toothpick.

For the angels, cut each bacon slice lengthwise in half and gently stretch with the back of a knife. Wrap a bacon strip around each oyster and secure with a toothpick.

Put the devils and angels onto a baking sheet and cook in the preheated oven for 10–15 minutes until sizzling hot and the bacon is cooked. Serve hot.

makes 16 | *prep 20 minutes* | *cook 10 minutes*

SHRIMP WRAPPED IN HAM

16 thin slices serrano ham or
    prosciutto
16 raw jumbo shrimp, shelled and
    deveined but tails left intact
extra virgin olive oil, for rubbing

TOMATO-CAPER DRESSING
2 tomatoes, peeled and seeded
1 small red onion, very finely chopped
4 tbsp very finely chopped fresh
    parsley
1 tbsp capers, rinsed
finely grated rind of 1 large lemon
4 tbsp extra virgin olive oil
1 tbsp sherry vinegar

Preheat the oven to 325°F/160°C.
Meanwhile, make the dressing. Finely chop
the tomato flesh and put in a bowl. Add
the onion, parsley, capers, and lemon rind
and gently toss together. Combine the oil
and vinegar, then add to the other
dressing ingredients. Mix together, cover,
and set aside.

Wrap a slice of ham around each shrimp
and rub with a little oil. Put the shrimp in a
heatproof dish large enough to hold them
in a single layer. Bake in the preheated
oven for 10 minutes.

Transfer the shrimp to a serving platter
and spoon over the dressing. Serve at
once, or let cool to room temperature
before serving.

serves 8 | prep 10 minutes | cook 3–4 minutes

SIZZLING CHILI SHRIMP

1 lb 2 oz/500 g raw jumbo shrimp,
  in their shells
1 small fresh red chili
6 tbsp Spanish olive oil
2 garlic cloves, finely chopped
pinch of paprika
pinch of salt
crusty bread, to serve

To prepare the shrimp, pull off their heads, then peel off their shells, leaving the tails intact. Using a sharp knife, make a shallow slit along the underside of each shrimp, then pull out the dark vein and discard. Rinse the shrimp under cold running water and dry well on paper towels.

Cut the chili in half lengthwise, remove and discard the seeds, and finely chop the flesh. Wear gloves while you do this or wash your hands very thoroughly afterward, because chili juice can cause irritation to sensitive skin, especially around the eyes, nose, or mouth. Whatever you do, don't rub your eyes after touching the cut flesh of a chili.

Heat the oil in a large, heavy-bottom skillet or ovenproof casserole over medium heat, add the garlic, and cook for 30 seconds, stirring. Add the shrimp, chili, paprika, and salt and cook for 2–3 minutes, stirring constantly, until the shrimp turn pink and begin to curl.

Serve the shrimp in the cooking dish, still sizzling. Accompany with toothpicks, to spear the shrimp, and chunks or slices of crusty bread to mop up the aromatic cooking oil.

serves 4 | *prep* 10 minutes | *cook* 4–6 minutes

SESAME SHRIMP TOASTS

8 oz/225 g raw shrimp, shelled and
 deveined
2 tbsp lard or vegetable shortening
1 egg white, lightly beaten
1 tsp chopped scallions
1/2 tsp finely chopped fresh gingerroot
1 tbsp Chinese rice wine or dry sherry
1 tsp cornstarch
2 tsp water
6 slices white bread, crusts removed
5 oz/140 g sesame seeds
peanut oil, for deep-frying
salt and pepper

Put the shrimp and lard on a cutting board
and chop them together until they form a
paste. Scrape into a bowl and stir
in the egg white, scallions, ginger,
and rice wine. Mix the cornstarch and
water together in a small bowl until a
smooth paste forms, then stir into the
shrimp mixture and season to taste with
salt and pepper.

Spread the shrimp paste evenly over one
side of each slice of bread. Spread out the
sesame seeds on a large, flat plate, or tray
and gently press the spread side of each
slice of bread into the seeds to coat.

Heat the oil in a preheated wok or large,
heavy-bottom skillet. Add half the slices of
bread, spread-side down, and cook for
2–3 minutes until golden brown. Remove
with a slotted spoon and drain on paper
towels. Cook the remaining slices in the
same way. Cut each slice into fingers and
serve at once.

makes 25 | prep 15 minutes | cook 10–15 minutes

DEEP-FRIED SHRIMP BALLS

10 oz/280 g raw shrimp, shelled and
  deveined
1-inch/2.5-cm piece fresh gingerroot,
  coarsely chopped
1½ cups bean sprouts, coarsely
  chopped
1 bunch of scallions, coarsely chopped
generous ¾ cup all-purpose flour
1 tsp baking powder
1 egg, lightly beaten
½ tsp sambal oelek
pinch of salt
1–2 tbsp lukewarm water, if needed
peanut or sunflower-seed oil, for
  deep-frying
dip of your choice, to serve (optional)

Put the shrimp, ginger, bean sprouts, and
scallions in a food processor and process
until finely chopped, scraping down the
sides of the mixing bowl once or twice.
Scrape the mixture into a bowl and add
the flour, baking powder, egg, sambal
oelek, and salt. Mix thoroughly with your
hands until a firm mixture forms, adding
a little of the water if necessary.

Heat the oil in a deep-fat fryer, large,
heavy-bottom pan, or wok to
350–375°F/180–190°C, or until a cube of
bread browns in 30 seconds.

Meanwhile, shape spoonfuls of the shrimp
mixture into walnut-size balls with your
hands. Deep-fry the shrimp balls in small
batches for 2–3 minutes until golden
brown (if you deep-fry too many balls at
one time, the oil temperature will drop and
they will be soggy). Remove with a slotted
spoon and drain on paper towels. If
serving hot, serve at once, or let cool
to room temperature. Serve with a dip,
if desired.

makes 16 | prep 15 minutes | cook 5–10 minutes

JUMBO SHRIMP
WITH SWEET & SOUR SAUCE

DIP
1 small fresh red Thai chili, seeded
1 tsp honey
4 tbsp soy sauce

ROLLS
2 tbsp fresh cilantro leaves
1 garlic clove
1½ tsp Thai Red Curry Paste
16 won ton skins
1 egg white, lightly beaten
16 raw jumbo shrimp, shelled and
   deveined but with tails left intact
sunflower-seed oil, for deep-frying

To make the dip, finely chop the chili, then mix with the honey and soy in a small serving bowl and stir well. Cover and set aside.

To make the shrimp rolls, finely chop the cilantro and garlic, then mix with the curry paste in a bowl.

Spread the won ton skins out on a counter. Brush each won ton skin with egg white and put a small dab of the cilantro mixture in the center. Put a shrimp on top.

Fold the won ton skin over, enclosing the shrimp but leaving the tail exposed. Repeat with the other shrimp.

Heat the oil in a deep-fat fryer, large, heavy-bottom pan, or wok to 350–375°F/180–190°C, or until a cube of bread browns in 30 seconds. Deep-fry the shrimp in small batches for 1–2 minutes until golden brown and crisp (if you deep-fry too many shrimp at one time, the oil temperature will drop and they will be soggy). Drain on paper towels and serve with the dip.

serves 8 | *prep* 30 minutes | *cook* 15 minutes

MUSSELS WITH HERB & GARLIC BUTTER

1 lb 12 oz/800 g live mussels
splash of dry white wine
1 bay leaf
6 tbsp butter
5/8 cup fresh white or brown
   bread crumbs
4 tbsp chopped fresh flat-leaf parsley,
   plus extra sprigs to garnish
2 tbsp snipped fresh chives
2 garlic cloves, finely chopped
salt and pepper
lemon wedges, to serve

Preheat the oven to 450°F/230°C. Clean the mussels by scrubbing or scraping the shells and pulling out any beards that are attached to them. Discard any with broken shells and any that refuse to close when tapped. Put the mussels in a colander and rinse well under cold running water.

Put the mussels in a large pan and add the wine and bay leaf. Cook, covered, over high heat, shaking the pan occasionally, for 3–4 minutes, or until the mussels have opened. Discard any mussels that remain closed. Strain the mussels.

Shell the mussels, reserving one half of each shell. Arrange the mussels, in their half shells, in a large, shallow, ovenproof serving dish.

Melt the butter in a small pan and pour into a small bowl. Add the bread crumbs, parsley, chives, garlic, and salt and pepper to taste and mix together well. Leave until the butter has set slightly. Using your fingers or 2 teaspoons, take a large pinch of the butter mixture and use to fill each mussel shell, pressing it down well.

Bake the mussels in the preheated oven for 10 minutes, or until hot. Serve at once, garnished with parsley sprigs, and accompanied by lemon wedges for squeezing over.

makes 16 | prep 20 minutes | cook 25–35 minutes

CARIBBEAN CRAB CAKES

1 potato, peeled and cut into chunks
pinch of salt
4 scallions, chopped
1 garlic clove, chopped
1 tbsp chopped fresh thyme
1 tbsp chopped fresh basil
1 tbsp chopped fresh cilantro
8 oz/225 g white crabmeat, drained if
   canned and thawed if frozen
1/2 tsp Dijon mustard
1/2 fresh green chili, seeded and
   finely chopped
1 egg, lightly beaten
all-purpose flour, for dusting
sunflower-seed oil, for pan-frying
pepper
lime wedges, to garnish
dip or salsa of your choice, to serve

Put the potato in a small pan and add water to cover and the salt. Bring to a boil, then reduce the heat, cover, and let simmer for 10–15 minutes until softened. Drain well, turn into a large bowl, and mash with a potato masher or fork until smooth.

Meanwhile, put the scallions, garlic, thyme, basil, and cilantro in a mortar and pound with a pestle until smooth. Add the herb paste to the mashed potato with the crabmeat, mustard, chili, egg, and pepper to taste. Mix well, cover with plastic wrap, and let chill in the refrigerator for 30 minutes.

Sprinkle flour onto a large, flat plate. Shape spoonfuls of the crabmeat mixture into small balls with your hands, then flatten slightly and dust with flour, shaking off any excess. Heat the oil in a skillet over high heat, add the crab cakes, and cook in batches for 2–3 minutes on each side until golden. Remove with a slotted spoon and drain on paper towels. Set aside to cool to room temperature.

Arrange the crab cakes on a serving dish and garnish with lime wedges. Serve with a bowl of dip or salsa.

makes 24 | prep 20 minutes | cook 15 minutes

SEAFOOD PHYLLO PACKAGES

Preheat the oven to 400°F/200°C. Remove and discard the skin and bones from the salmon, put in a bowl, and gently flake with a fork. Remove and discard any cartilage from the crabmeat, put in a separate bowl, and gently flake with a fork. Divide the parsley and scallions between the bowls and mix well together.

Lay a sheet of phyllo pastry out on a counter, brush with melted butter, then place a second sheet on top, keeping the remaining sheets covered with a damp dish towel. Cut into 4-inch/10-cm squares. Place a teaspoonful of the salmon mixture on each square. Brush the edges of the pastry with melted butter, then draw together to make little pouches. Pinch together to seal. Repeat with 2 more sheets of phyllo and the salmon mixture, then repeat with the remaining sheets of phyllo and the crabmeat mixture.

Lightly oil a baking sheet and put the packages on it. Bake in the preheated oven for 15 minutes until golden. Serve warm.

3¹/₂ oz/100 g canned red salmon,
   drained
3¹/₂ oz/100 g canned crabmeat,
   drained
2 tbsp chopped fresh parsley
8 scallions, finely chopped
8 sheets phyllo pastry (about 8 x 12
   inches/20 x 30 cm), thawed if frozen
melted butter, for brushing
sunflower-seed oil, for oiling

makes 24 | *prep* 20 minutes | *cook* 10–18 minutes

CRISPY CRAB WON TONS

6 oz/175 g white crabmeat, drained if
  canned and thawed if frozen, flaked
1³/4 oz/50 g canned water chestnuts,
  drained, rinsed and chopped
1 small fresh red chili, chopped
1 scallion, chopped
1 tbsp cornstarch
1 tsp dry sherry
1 tsp light soy sauce
¹/2 tsp lime juice
24 won ton skins
vegetable oil, for deep-frying
lime slices, to garnish

To make the filling, mix the crabmeat, water
chestnuts, chili, scallion, cornstarch, sherry,
soy sauce, and lime juice together in
a bowl.

Spread the won ton skins out on a counter
and spoon an equal portion of the filling into
the center of each won ton skin.

Dampen the edges of the won ton skins with
a little water and fold them in half to form
triangles. Fold the 2 pointed ends in toward
the center, moisten with a little water to
secure, then pinch together to seal.

Heat the oil in a deep-fat fryer, large, heavy-
bottom pan, or wok to 350–375°F/180–190°C,
or until a cube of bread browns in 30 seconds.
Deep-fry the won tons in batches for
2–3 minutes until golden brown and crisp (if
you deep-fry too many won tons at one time,
the oil temperature will drop and they will be
soggy). Remove with a slotted spoon and
drain on paper towels.

Serve the won tons hot, garnished with
lime slices.

3

Looking for something light and elegant to serve as a first course? Fish is the perfect solution, full of fresh, natural flavor, as well as subtle, inviting color—especially when teamed with bright green herbs and vibrant lemon or lime wedges. And it's a winner whether the dish is simplicity itself or a little more elaborate.

FISH FIRST

Nothing could be simpler to prepare than Gravadlax—it only needs time to develop its delicious flavor. Ceviche is another refrigerator classic, which really packs a punch. But those bistro favorites Moules Marinière, Calamares, and Thai Fish Cakes are hard to beat. However, if you are out to impress, Salmon Tartare is seriously sophisticated, Noodle-Wrapped Teriyaki Fish stylish, and Chèvre & Oyster Tartlets outrageously upmarket.

serves 8 | *prep* 10 minutes | *cook* 15 minutes

SMOKED FISH PATE

2 lb/900 g undyed kippered herring
   fillets
2 garlic cloves, finely chopped
¾ cup olive oil
6 tbsp light cream
salt and pepper
lemon slices, to garnish
crackers, to serve

Put the kippered herrings in a large skillet or
fish poacher and add cold water to just cover.
Bring to a boil, then immediately reduce the
heat and poach gently for 10 minutes until
tender. If using a skillet, you may need to do
this in batches.

Transfer the fish to a cutting board using
a spatula. Remove and discard the skin.
Coarsely flake the flesh with a fork and
remove and discard any remaining tiny
bones. Transfer the fish to a pan over low
heat, add the garlic, and break up the fish
with a wooden spoon.

Gradually add the oil, beating well after
each addition. Add the cream and beat until
smooth, but do not allow the mixture to boil.

Remove the pan from the heat and season
to taste with salt, if necessary, and pepper.
Spoon the pâté into a serving dish, cover,
and set aside to cool completely. Let chill
in the refrigerator until required, for up to
3 days.

Garnish with lemon slices and serve
with crackers.

makes 4 | prep 10 minutes | cook 20–25 minutes

TUNA STUFFED TOMATOES

4 plum tomatoes
2 tbsp sun-dried tomato paste
4 oz/115 g canned tuna, drained
2 tbsp capers, rinsed
salt and pepper

MAYONNAISE
2 egg yolks
2 tsp lemon juice
finely grated rind of 1 lemon
4 tbsp olive oil

TO GARNISH
2 sun-dried tomatoes, cut into strips
fresh basil leaves

Preheat the oven to 400°F/200°C. Halve the fresh tomatoes, scoop out the seeds, and discard. Divide the sun-dried tomato paste between the tomato halves and spread around the inside of the tomato shells.

Put on a baking sheet and roast in the preheated oven for 12–15 minutes. Let cool slightly.

Meanwhile, make the mayonnaise. Put the egg yolks and lemon juice and rind in a blender or food processor and process until smooth. With the motor running, very slowly add the oil through the feed tube. Stop the machine as soon as the mayonnaise has thickened. Alternatively, use a hand whisk, beating the mixture constantly until it thickens.

Flake the tuna with a fork, then stir into the mayonnaise with the capers and salt and pepper to taste.

Spoon the tuna mayonnaise mixture into the tomato shells and garnish with sun-dried tomato strips and basil leaves. Return to the oven for a few minutes to heat through before serving or serve chilled.

serves 8-12 | *prep 10 minutes, plus 2 days' chilling* | *cook no cooking required*

GRAVADLAX

Rinse the salmon fillets under cold running water and dry with paper towels. Put 1 fillet, skin-side down, in a nonmetallic dish.

Mix the dill, sea salt, sugar, and peppercorns together in a small bowl. Spread this mixture over the fillet in the dish and put the second fillet, skin-side up, on top. Put a plate, the same size as the fish, on top and weight down with 3–4 food cans.

Let chill in the refrigerator for 2 days, turning the fish about every 12 hours and basting with any juices that come out of the fish.

Remove the salmon from the brine and thinly slice, without slicing the skin, as you would smoked salmon. Cut the buttered bread into triangles and serve with the salmon. Garnish with lemon wedges and dill sprigs.

2 salmon fillets, with skin on, about
    1 lb/450 g each
6 tbsp coarsely chopped fresh dill
³/₈ cup sea salt
¹/₄ cup sugar
1 tbsp white peppercorns, coarsely
    crushed
12 slices brown bread, buttered,
    to serve

TO GARNISH
lemon slices
fresh dill sprigs

serves 4 | *prep* 15 minutes, plus 30 minutes' chilling | *cook* 20 minutes

THAI FISH CAKES

Put the cod in a food processor and process until coarsely chopped. Add the curry paste, egg, sugar, salt, and cornstarch and process until well blended.

Stir in the beans and cilantro.

Transfer to a bowl, cover with plastic wrap, and chill in the refrigerator for 30 minutes.

Remove from the refrigerator, shape the fish mixture into 12 balls with your hands, then flatten each ball into a 2-inch/5-cm cake.

1 lb 2 oz/500 g skinless, boneless
   cod fillet, cut into chunks
1 tbsp Thai Red Curry Paste
1 egg, beaten
1 tsp brown sugar
1 tsp salt
1 tbsp cornstarch
2³/₄ oz/75 g green beans,
   finely chopped
1 tbsp chopped fresh cilantro
4 tbsp vegetable oil
lime wedges, to garnish

TO SERVE
salad
stir-fried green vegetables,
   such as green beans, broccoli,
   and snow peas

Heat the oil in a skillet over medium heat, add the fish cakes, and cook in batches for 3 minutes on each side, or until golden brown and cooked through. Keep warm in a low oven while cooking the remainder.

Garnish with lime wedges and serve with salad or stir-fried green vegetables such as green beans, snow peas, or broccoli.

serves 4 | *prep* 15 minutes, plus 20 minutes' chilling | *cook* 20 minutes

NOODLE-WRAPPED TERIYAKI FISH

2 boneless salmon steaks, about
6 oz/175 g each and about 3/4 inch/
2 cm thick, skinned
bottled teriyaki sauce
12 large spinach leaves, rinsed
and dried with any tough stems
removed, or about 36 young
spinach leaves
48 long, fresh medium Chinese
egg noodles

Using a sharp knife, cut the salmon steaks into
1-inch/2.5-cm pieces.

Brush the top of each fish piece with teriyaki
sauce. Working with 1 spinach leaf at a time, lay
it out on a counter, bottom-side up, with the
stem end facing you. Place a piece of fish, sauce-
side down, in the center of the leaf. Fold the
sides inward to overlap, then roll up from the
bottom so that the fish is enclosed. Continue
wrapping the remaining fish pieces. Wrap each
spinach package with 2 noodles, from side to
side, then repeat with 2 more noodles, wrapped
at right angles. Have all the dangling loose
noodle ends on the bottom, then cut off the
excess and press the ends together. Cover and
let chill in the refrigerator for at least 20 minutes
or up to 8 hours.

To cook, place a bamboo steamer over a pan of
boiling water. Put as many fish packages as will
fit in a single layer in the steamer, cover, and let
steam for 10 minutes. Serve at once, while you
steam any remaining packages.

serves 4 | prep 20 minutes, plus 48 hours' marinating | cook no cooking required

SALMON TARTARE

Put the salmon in a shallow, nonmetallic dish. Combine the sea salt, sugar, and chopped dill in a small bowl, then rub the mixture into the fish until well coated. Season to taste with pepper. Cover with plastic wrap and let chill in the refrigerator for at least 48 hours, turning the salmon once.

Put the tarragon in a bowl with the mustard, lemon juice, and salt and pepper to taste. Remove the salmon from the refrigerator, chop into small pieces, and add to the bowl. Stir until the salmon is well coated.

To make the topping, put all the topping ingredients in a separate bowl and mix well together. Put a 4-inch/10-cm steel cooking ring or round cookie cutter on each of 4 small serving plates. Divide the salmon between the 4 steel rings so that each ring is half full. Level the surface of each one, then top with the cream cheese mixture. Smooth the surfaces, then carefully remove the steel rings. Garnish with dill sprigs and serve.

1 lb 2 oz/500 g salmon fillet, skinned
2 tbsp sea salt
1 tbsp superfine sugar
2 tbsp chopped fresh dill, plus extra
  sprigs to garnish
1 tbsp chopped fresh tarragon
1 tsp Dijon mustard
juice of 1 lemon
salt and pepper

TOPPING
1³/₄ cups cream cheese
1 tbsp snipped fresh chives
pinch of paprika

serves 4–6 | prep 15 minutes, plus 1–2 hours' marinating | cook 10 minutes

ANGLER FISH, ROSEMARY & BACON SKEWERS

12 oz/350 g angler fish tail or
  9 oz/250 g angler fish fillet
12 fresh rosemary stems
3 tbsp Spanish olive oil
juice of ¹/₂ small lemon
1 garlic clove, crushed
6 rindless thick Canadian bacon slices
salt and pepper
lemon wedges, to garnish
aïoli, to serve

If using angler fish tail, cut either side of the central bone with a sharp knife and remove the flesh to form 2 fillets. Slice the fillets in half lengthwise, then cut each fillet into 12 bite-size chunks to give a total of 24 pieces. Put the angler fish pieces in a large bowl.

To prepare the rosemary skewers, strip the leaves off the stems and set them aside, leaving a few leaves at one end.

For the marinade, finely chop the reserved leaves and whisk with the oil, lemon juice, garlic, and salt and pepper to taste in a nonmetallic bowl. Add the angler fish pieces and toss until coated in the marinade. Cover and let marinate in the refrigerator for 1–2 hours.

Cut each bacon slice in half lengthwise, then in half widthwise, and roll up each piece. Thread 2 angler fish pieces alternately with 2 bacon rolls onto the prepared rosemary skewers.

Preheat the broiler, griddle, or barbecue. If you are cooking the skewers under a broiler, arrange them on the broiler rack so that the leaves of the rosemary skewers protrude from the broiler and therefore do not catch fire during cooking. Cook the angler fish and bacon skewers, turning frequently and basting with any remaining marinade, for 10 minutes, or until cooked. Serve hot, garnished with lemon wedges for squeezing over, and accompanied by a bowl of aïoli for dipping.

SHRIMP COCKTAIL

½ iceberg lettuce, finely shredded
⅔ cup mayonnaise
2 tbsp light cream
2 tbsp tomato ketchup
few drops of Tabasco sauce,
  or to taste
juice of ½ lemon, or to taste
6 oz/175 g cooked shelled shrimp
salt and pepper
thin buttered brown bread slices,
  to serve

TO GARNISH
paprika, for sprinkling
4 cooked shrimp, in their shells
4 lemon slices

Divide the lettuce between 4 small serving dishes (traditionally, stemmed glass ones, but any small dishes will be fine).

Mix the mayonnaise, cream, and tomato ketchup together in a bowl. Add the Tabasco sauce and lemon juice and season well with salt and pepper.

Divide the shelled shrimp equally between the dishes and pour over the dressing. Cover and let chill in the refrigerator for 30 minutes.

Sprinkle a little paprika over the cocktails and garnish each dish with a shrimp and a lemon slice. Serve the cocktails with slices of brown bread and butter.

serves 4 | prep 15 minutes, plus 8 hours' marinating | cook 8–12 minutes

SHRIMP SATAY

12 raw jumbo shrimp, shelled but with
  tails left intact

MARINADE
1 tsp ground coriander
1 tsp ground cumin
2 tbsp light soy sauce
4 tbsp vegetable oil
1 tbsp curry powder
1 tbsp ground turmeric
1/2 cup canned coconut milk
3 tbsp sugar

PEANUT SAUCE
2 tbsp vegetable oil
3 garlic cloves, crushed
1 tbsp Thai Red Curry Paste
1/2 cup canned coconut milk
1 cup fish or chicken stock
1 tbsp sugar
1 tsp salt
1 tbsp lemon juice
4 tbsp unsalted roasted peanuts,
  finely chopped
4 tbsp dried white bread crumbs

Using a sharp knife, make a shallow slit along the underside of each shrimp, then pull out the dark vein and discard. Set aside. Mix the marinade ingredients together in a bowl and add the shrimp. Mix well together, cover, and let marinate in the refrigerator for at least 8 hours or overnight.

To make the sauce, heat the oil in a large skillet over high heat. Add the garlic and cook, stirring, until just starting to color. Add the curry paste and cook,

stirring, for an additional 30 seconds. Add the coconut milk, stock, sugar, salt, and lemon juice and stir well. Boil for 1–2 minutes, stirring constantly. Add the peanuts and bread crumbs and mix well together. Pour into a bowl, cover, and set aside.

Preheat the broiler or barbecue. Thread 3 shrimp onto each of 4 skewers. Cook under or over high heat for 3–4 minutes on each side until just cooked through. Serve at once with the peanut sauce.

serves 4 | prep 25 minutes | cook 5 minutes

MOULES MARINIERE

4 lb 8 oz/2 kg live mussels
1¼ cups dry white wine
6 shallots, finely chopped
1 bouquet garni
pepper
crusty bread, to serve

Clean the mussels by scrubbing or scraping the shells and pulling out any beards that are attached to them. Discard any with broken shells or any that refuse to close when tapped. Put the mussels in a colander and rinse well under cold running water.

Pour the wine into a large, heavy-bottom pan, add the shallots and bouquet garni, and season to taste with pepper. Bring to a boil over medium heat. Add the mussels, cover tightly, and cook, shaking the pan occasionally, for 3–4 minutes, or until the mussels have opened. Remove and discard the bouquet garni and any mussels that remain closed.

Divide the mussels between 4 soup plates with a slotted spoon. Tilt the pan to let any sand settle, then spoon the cooking liquid over the mussels. Serve at once with bread.

serves 4 | *prep* 25 minutes, plus 2 hours' chilling | *cook* no cooking required

CEVICHE

8 live scallops, shucked
16 large raw shrimp, in shells
2 sea bass fillets, about 5¹/₂ oz/150 g
  each, skinned
1 large lemon
1 lime
1 red onion, thinly sliced
¹/₂ fresh red chili, seeded and finely
  chopped
2–4 tbsp extra virgin olive oil

TO SERVE
salad greens
lime or lemon wedges
pepper

Scrub the scallops under cold running water. Using a strong knife, prise the shells open. Remove and discard the gray beard that surrounds each scallop and the black thread and stomach bag. Detach the scallop and coral from each shell with a spoon and separate the coral from the scallop. Rinse under cold running water and dry with paper towels. Slice the scallops into 2–3 horizontal slices each, depending on the size. Put in a nonmetallic bowl with the corals.

Pull off the heads of the shrimp, then peel off their shells. Using a sharp knife, make a shallow slit in the underside of each shrimp, then pull out the dark vein and discard. Rinse the shrimp under cold running water and dry well on paper towels. Add to the scallops.

Cut the sea bass into thin slices across the grain and add to the shellfish.

Cut the lemon in half and squeeze the juice over the fish. Repeat with the lime.

Gently stir to coat the seafood well in the citrus juices, then cover and let chill in the refrigerator for 2 hours, or until the seafood becomes opaque, but do not leave for longer or the seafood will be too soft.

Using a slotted spoon, transfer the seafood to a separate bowl. Add the onion, chili, and oil and gently stir together. Let stand for 5 minutes.

Spoon onto individual plates and serve with salad greens, lemon or lime wedges, and pepper.

makes 12 | *prep 20 minutes, plus 45 minutes' chilling* | *cook 20 minutes*

CHEVRE & OYSTER TARTLETS

scant 1 cup all-purpose flour, plus
    extra for dusting
pinch of salt
5 tbsp butter, diced, plus extra for
    greasing
1 egg yolk
1 onion, chopped
12 live oysters, shucked
2 tbsp chopped fresh flat-leaf parsley,
    plus extra sprigs to garnish
salt and pepper
7 oz/200 g goat cheese, crumbled

Grease 12 x 2¾-inch/7-cm tartlet pans. Sift
the flour and salt together into a bowl. Rub
4 tbsp of the butter into the flour until fine
crumbs form. Mix in the egg yolk to make
a dough. Add a little cold water if needed.
Shape into a ball and turn out onto a lightly
floured counter. Roll out to a thickness of
¼ inch/5 mm. Line the prepared pans with
the dough and trim the edges. Cover and let
chill in the refrigerator for 45 minutes.

Preheat the oven to 400°F/200°C. Remove
the tartlet shells from the refrigerator and
bake in the preheated oven for 10 minutes
until golden.

Meanwhile, heat the remaining butter in a pan
over medium heat, add the onion, and cook,
stirring frequently for 4 minutes. Add the
oysters, parsley, and salt and pepper to taste
and cook, stirring, for 1 minute.

Remove the tartlet shells from the oven.
Divide half of the goat cheese between them.
Top with the oyster mixture, crumble over
the remaining cheese, then bake for an
additional 10 minutes. Garnish with parsley
sprigs and serve hot.

serves 8 | prep 25 minutes | cook 35 minutes

SCALLOPS IN SAFFRON SAUCE

²/₃ cup dry white wine
²/₃ cup fish stock
large pinch of saffron threads
2 lb/900 g shucked live scallops,
   preferably large ones
3 tbsp Spanish olive oil
1 small onion, finely chopped
2 garlic cloves, finely chopped
²/₃ cup heavy cream
squeeze of lemon juice
salt and pepper
chopped fresh flat-leaf parsley,
   to garnish
crusty bread, to serve

Put the wine, stock, and saffron in a pan over medium heat and bring to a boil. Reduce the heat, cover, and let simmer gently for 15 minutes.

Remove and discard the gray beard that surrounds each scallop and the black thread and stomach bag. Detach the scallop and coral from each shell with a spoon. Rinse under cold running water and dry with paper towels. Slice the scallops horizontally into thick slices, including the corals. Season to taste with salt and pepper.

Heat the oil in a large, heavy-bottom skillet over medium heat. Add the onion and garlic and cook, stirring frequently, for 5 minutes, or until softened and lightly browned. Add the sliced scallops and cook gently, stirring occasionally, for 5 minutes, or until they just turn opaque. Do not overcook the scallops or they will become tough and rubbery.

Using a slotted spoon, transfer the scallops to a warmed plate. Add the saffron liquid to the pan, bring to a boil, and boil rapidly until reduced by about half. Reduce the heat and gradually stir in the cream, just a little at a time. Let simmer gently until the sauce thickens.

Return the scallops to the pan and let simmer in the sauce for 1–2 minutes just to heat them through. Add the lemon juice and season to taste with salt and pepper. Serve the scallops hot, garnished with chopped parsley, and accompanied by chunks or slices of crusty bread to mop up the saffron sauce.

serves 4–6 | *prep 10–25 minutes, plus 1–2 hours' chilling* | *cook 10 minutes*

POTTED CRAB

1 large cooked crab, prepared
  if possible
whole nutmeg, for grating
2 pinches of cayenne pepper or mace
juice of 1 lemon, or to taste
1 cup lightly salted butter
salt and pepper

TO SERVE
buttered toast slices
lemon wedges

If the crab is not already prepared, pick out
all the white and brown meat, taking great
care to remove all the meat from the claws.

Mix the white and brown meat together in
a bowl, but do not mash too smoothly.
Season well with salt and pepper and add
a good grating of nutmeg, the cayenne
pepper, and lemon juice.

Melt half the butter in a pan over medium
heat and carefully stir in the crabmeat.
Turn the mixture out into 4–6 small soufflé
dishes or ramekins.

Melt the remaining butter in a clean pan
over medium heat, then continue heating
for a few moments until it stops bubbling.
Allow the sediment to settle, then carefully
pour the clarified butter over the crab
mixture. Cover and let chill in the refrigerator
for at least 1 hour before serving with
buttered toast and lemon wedges. The seal
of clarified butter allows the potted crab to
be kept for 1–2 days.

serves 6 | prep 10 minutes | cook 8–12 minutes

CALAMARES

1 lb/450 g prepared squid
all-purpose flour, for coating
sunflower-seed oil, for deep-frying
salt
lemon wedges, to garnish
aïoli, to serve

Slice the squid into ½-inch/1-cm rings and halve the tentacles if large. Rinse under cold running water and dry well with paper towels. Dust the squid rings with flour so that they are lightly coated.

Heat the oil in a deep-fat fryer, large, heavy-bottom pan, or wok to 350–375°F/180–190°C, or until a cube of bread browns in 30 seconds. Deep-fry the squid rings in small batches for 2–3 minutes, or until golden brown and crisp all over, turning several times (if you deep-fry too many squid rings at one time, the oil temperature will drop and they will be soggy). Do not overcook as the squid will become tough and rubbery rather than moist and tender.

Remove with a slotted spoon and drain well on paper towels. Keep warm in a low oven while you deep-fry the remaining squid rings.

Sprinkle the fried squid rings with salt and serve piping hot, garnished with lemon wedges for squeezing over. Accompany with a bowl of aïoli for dipping.

4

When it comes to soups and stews, fish's famed diversity and versatility really come into their own. Fish offers the whole range of eating experience, from the smooth, creamy, and subtly flavored to the hearty, chunky, and spicy, with all the glorious variations in between. And all this cooked in one pot and served in one bowl!

SOUPS AND STEWS

The recipe titles in this chapter read like a Who's Who of the world's great cuisines—New England Clam Chowder, Bouillabaisse, Louisiana Gumbo, Corn & Crab Soup, and Shrimp Laksa. But there are other, less well-known regional delights besides—Spanish Swordfish Stew, Mexican Fish & Roasted Tomato Soup, and the fragrant Breton Fish Soup with Cider & Sorrel.

serves 4 | prep 15 minutes, plus 30 minutes' marinating | cook 40 minutes

COD & SWEET POTATO SOUP

4 tbsp lemon juice
1 fresh red chili, seeded and
    finely sliced
pinch of nutmeg
9 oz/250 g cod fillets, skinned, rinsed,
    and dried
1 tbsp vegetable oil
1 onion, chopped
4 scallions, chopped
2 garlic cloves, chopped
1 lb/450 g sweet potatoes, diced
4 cups vegetable stock
1 carrot, sliced
5¹/₂ oz/150 g white cabbage,
    shredded
2 celery stalks, sliced
salt and pepper
crusty bread, to serve

Put the lemon juice, chili, and nutmeg in a shallow, nonmetallic dish and mix together. Cut the cod into chunks and add to the dish. Turn in the marinade until well coated. Cover with plastic wrap and let marinate in the refrigerator for 30 minutes.

Heat the oil in a large pan over medium heat. Add the onion and scallions and cook, stirring frequently, for 4 minutes. Add the garlic and cook, stirring, for 2 minutes.

Add the sweet potatoes, stock, and salt and pepper to taste. Bring to a boil, then reduce the heat, cover, and let simmer for 10 minutes. Add the carrot, cabbage, and celery, season again, and simmer for 8–10 minutes.

Let the soup cool slightly, then transfer to a blender or food processor and process until smooth, working in batches if necessary. Return to the pan. Add the fish and marinade and bring gently to a boil. Reduce the heat and let simmer for 10 minutes. Ladle the soup into bowls and serve with crusty bread.

serves 4 | prep 15 minutes | cook 30–35 minutes

GARLIC FISH SOUP

2 tsp olive oil
1 large onion, chopped
1 small fennel bulb, chopped
1 leek, sliced
3–4 large garlic cloves, thinly sliced
1/2 cup dry white wine
5 cups fish stock
4 tbsp white rice
1 strip of thinly pared lemon rind
1 bay leaf
1 lb/450 g skinless white fish fillets,
    cut into 11/2-inch/4-cm pieces
1/4 cup heavy cream
salt and pepper
2 tbsp chopped fresh parsley, to
    garnish

Heat the oil in a large pan over medium–low heat. Add the onion, fennel, leek, and garlic and cook, stirring frequently, for 4–5 minutes until the onion is softened.

Add the wine and let the mixture bubble briefly. Add the stock, rice, lemon rind, and bay leaf. Bring to a boil, then reduce the heat to medium–low and let simmer for 20–25 minutes until the rice and vegetables are soft. Remove and discard the lemon rind and bay leaf.

Let the soup cool slightly, then transfer to a blender or food processor and process until smooth, working in batches if necessary. (If using a food processor, strain off the cooking liquid and set aside. Purée the solids with enough cooking liquid to moisten them, then combine with the remaining liquid.)

Return the soup to the pan and bring to a simmer. Add the fish to the soup, cover, and let simmer gently, stirring occasionally, for an additional 4–5 minutes until the fish is cooked and begins to flake.

Stir in the cream. Taste and adjust the seasoning, adding salt, if necessary, and pepper. Ladle into warmed bowls and serve sprinkled with chopped parsley.

serves 4 | prep 15 minutes | cook 35 minutes

BRETON FISH SOUP
WITH CIDER & SORREL

2 tsp butter
1 large leek, thinly sliced
2 shallots, finely chopped
1/2 cup hard cider
1 1/4 cups fish stock
9 oz/250 g potatoes, diced
1 bay leaf
4 tbsp all-purpose flour
scant 1 cup milk
scant 1 cup heavy cream
2 oz/55 g sorrel leaves
12 oz/350 g skinless angler fish or cod
   fillets, cut into 1-inch/2.5-cm pieces
salt and pepper

Melt the butter in a large pan over medium–low heat. Add the leek and shallots, and cook, stirring frequently, for 5 minutes, or until they start to soften. Add the cider and bring to a boil.

Stir in the stock, potatoes, and bay leaf with a large pinch of salt (unless the stock is salty) and return to a boil. Reduce the heat, cover, and cook gently for 10 minutes.

Put the flour in a small bowl and very slowly whisk in a few tablespoons of the milk to make a thick paste. Stir in a little more milk to make a smooth liquid.

Adjust the heat so that the soup bubbles gently. Stir in the flour mixture and cook, stirring frequently, for 5 minutes. Add the remaining milk and half the cream. Cook for an additional 10 minutes, or until the potatoes are tender.

Finely chop the sorrel and combine with the remaining cream. (If using a food processor, add the sorrel and chop, then add the cream and process briefly.)

Stir the sorrel cream into the soup and add the fish. Cook, stirring occasionally, for an additional 3 minutes, or until the angler fish stiffens or the cod just begins to flake. Taste the soup and adjust the seasoning, if necessary. Ladle into warmed bowls and serve.

serves 4 | prep 15 minutes | cook 35 minutes

SAFFRON FISH SOUP

Melt the butter in a pan over medium heat, add the onion, leek, and carrot, and cook, stirring frequently, for 3–4 minutes until the onion is softened.

Add the saffron, rice, wine, and stock and bring just to a boil, then reduce the heat to low. Season to taste with salt and pepper. Cover and let simmer for 20 minutes, or until the rice and vegetables are tender.

Let the soup cool slightly, then transfer to a blender or food processor and process until smooth, working in batches if necessary. (If using a food processor, strain off the cooking liquid and set aside. Purée the solids with enough cooking liquid to moisten them, then combine with the remaining liquid.)

2 tsp butter
1 onion, finely chopped
1 leek, thinly sliced
1 carrot, thinly sliced
pinch of saffron threads
4 tbsp white rice
1/2 cup dry white wine
4 cups fish stock
1/2 cup heavy cream
12 oz/350 g skinless white fish fillets,
  such as cod, haddock, or angler fish,
  cut into 1/2-inch/1-cm cubes
4 tomatoes, peeled, seeded,
  and chopped
salt and pepper
3 tbsp snipped fresh chives, to garnish

Return to the pan, stir in the cream and let simmer over low heat for a few minutes until heated through, stirring occasionally.

Season the fish to taste with salt and pepper and add to the soup with the tomatoes. Cook for 3–5 minutes until the fish is just tender.

Stir in most of the chives. Taste the soup and adjust the seasoning, if necessary. Ladle into warmed shallow bowls, sprinkle the remaining chives on top, and serve.

serves 4 | *prep* 10 minutes | *cook* 25–30 minutes

MEXICAN FISH & ROASTED TOMATO SOUP

5 ripe tomatoes
5 garlic cloves, unpeeled
4 cups fish stock
1 lb 2 oz/500 g red snapper fillets,
   skinned and cut into chunks
2–3 tbsp olive oil
1 onion, chopped
2 fresh chilies, seeded and
   thinly sliced
lime wedges, to serve

Heat a dry, heavy-bottom skillet over high heat, add the tomatoes and garlic cloves, and cook, turning frequently, for 10–15 minutes until the skins are blackened and charred and the flesh is tender, or cook under a preheated hot broiler. Alternatively, put the tomatoes and garlic cloves in a roasting pan and bake in a preheated oven at 375–400°F/190–200°C for 40 minutes.

Let the tomatoes and garlic cool, then remove and discard the skins and coarsely chop the flesh, combining it with any juices from the pan. Set aside.

Heat the stock in a pan over medium heat until simmering, add the snapper, and cook just until opaque and slightly firm. Remove from the heat and set aside.

Heat the oil in a separate pan, add the onion and cook, stirring frequently, for 5 minutes until softened. Strain in the fish cooking liquid, then add the tomatoes and garlic and stir well.

Bring to a boil, then reduce the heat and let simmer for 5 minutes to combine the flavors. Add the chilies.

Divide chunks of the poached fish between 4 soup bowls, ladle over the hot soup, and serve with lime wedges for squeezing over.

serves 4–6 | prep 15 minutes | cook 1 hour

TROUT & CELERY ROOT SOUP

1 lb 9 oz/700 g whole trout, cleaned
7 oz/200 g celery root, peeled
  and diced
²/₃ cup heavy cream
3 tbsp cornstarch, dissolved in
  3 tbsp water
chopped fresh chervil or parsley,
  to garnish

FISH STOCK BASE
1 tbsp butter
l onion, thinly sliced
l carrot, thinly sliced
l leek, thinly sliced
1 cup dry white wine
5 cups water
1 bay leaf

To make the fish stock base, melt the butter in a fish poacher, a large pan or cast-iron casserole over medium–high heat, add the onion, carrot, and leek and cook for 3 minutes, or until the onion starts to soften.

Add the wine, water, and bay leaf. Bring to a boil, then reduce the heat a little, cover, and boil gently for 15 minutes.

Add the fish (cut the fish into pieces to fit, if necessary). Return to a boil and skim off any foam that rises to the surface. Reduce the heat to low and let simmer gently for 20 minutes.

Remove the fish with a slotted spoon and set aside. Strain the stock through a cheesecloth-lined strainer into a clean pan. Remove any fat from the stock. Bring the stock to a boil. Add the celery root

and boil gently, uncovered, for 15–20 minutes until it is tender and the liquid has reduced by about one third.

When the fish is cool enough to handle, peel off the skin and remove the flesh from the bones. Discard the skin, bones, head, and tail.

Add the cream to the soup and return to a boil. Stir in the dissolved cornstarch and boil gently, stirring frequently, for 2–3 minutes until slightly thickened. Return the fish to the soup and cook for 3–4 minutes to reheat. Taste and adjust the seasoning, if necessary. Ladle into warmed bowls and garnish with chervil or parsley.

serves 4 | prep 20 minutes | cook 15 minutes

THAI SHRIMP & SCALLOP SOUP

4 cups fish stock
juice of 1/2 lime
2 tbsp rice wine or sherry
1 leek, sliced
2 shallots, finely chopped
1 tbsp grated fresh gingerroot
1 fresh red chili, seeded and finely chopped
8 oz/225 g raw shrimp, shelled and deveined
8 oz/225 g live scallops, shucked and cleaned
1 1/2 tbsp chopped fresh flat-leaf parsley, plus extra to garnish
salt and pepper

Put the stock, lime juice, rice wine, leek, shallots, ginger, and chili in a large pan. Bring to a boil over high heat, then reduce the heat, cover, and let simmer for 10 minutes.

Add the shrimp, scallops, and parsley, season to taste with salt and pepper, and cook for 1–2 minutes.

Remove the pan from the heat and ladle the soup into warmed serving bowls. Garnish with chopped parsley and serve.

serves 4 | *prep 15 minutes, plus 10 minutes' cooling* | *cook 35 minutes*

SHRIMP & VEGETABLE BISQUE

3 tbsp butter
1 garlic clove, chopped
1 onion, sliced
1 carrot, chopped
1 celery stalk, sliced
5 cups fish stock
4 tbsp red wine
1 tbsp tomato paste
1 bay leaf
1 lb 5 oz/600 g raw shrimp, shelled
   and deveined
generous ⅓ cup heavy cream, plus
   extra to garnish
salt and pepper
cooked shrimp, in their shells,
   to garnish

Melt the butter in a large pan over medium heat. Add the garlic and onion and cook, stirring, for 3 minutes, until slightly softened. Add the carrot and celery and cook for an additional 3 minutes, stirring. Pour in the stock and wine, then add the tomato paste and bay leaf. Season to taste with salt and pepper. Bring to a boil, then reduce the heat and let simmer for 20 minutes. Remove from the heat and let cool for 10 minutes, then remove and discard the bay leaf.

Transfer half the soup to a blender or food processor and process until smooth, working in batches if necessary. Return to the pan with the remaining soup. Stir in the shelled shrimp and cook over low heat for 5–6 minutes.

Stir in the cream and cook for an additional 2 minutes, then remove from the heat and ladle into warmed serving bowls. Garnish with swirls of cream and shrimp. Serve at once.

serves 4 | *prep* 15 minutes | *cook* 30 minutes

MUSSEL SOUP

1 lb 10 oz/750 g live mussels,
  scrubbed and debearded
2 tbsp olive oil
7 tbsp butter
2 oz/55 g rindless lean
  bacon, chopped
1 onion, chopped
2 garlic cloves, finely chopped
generous 3/8 cup all-purpose flour
3 potatoes, thinly sliced
4 oz/115 g dried farfalle
1 1/4 cups heavy cream or
  panna da cucina
1 tbsp lemon juice
2 egg yolks
salt and pepper
2 tbsp finely chopped fresh parsley,
  to garnish

Bring a large, heavy-bottom pan of water to
a boil over high heat. Add the mussels, oil,
and pepper to taste. Cover tightly and cook,
shaking the pan occasionally, for 3–4 minutes,
or until the mussels have opened. Remove the
mussels with a slotted spoon, discarding any
that remain closed. Strain the cooking liquid
and set aside 5 cups. Remove the mussels
from their shells and set aside until required.

Melt the butter in a clean pan over low heat,
add the bacon, onion, and garlic and cook,
stirring occasionally, for 5 minutes. Stir in
the flour and cook, stirring constantly, for
1 minute. Gradually stir in all but
2 tablespoons of the reserved mussel
cooking liquid and bring to a boil, stirring
constantly. Add the potato slices and let
simmer for 5 minutes. Add the pasta and
let simmer for an additional 10 minutes.

Stir in the cream and lemon juice and season
to taste with salt and pepper. Add the
mussels. Mix the egg yolks and the remaining
mussel cooking liquid together in a pitcher,
then stir the mixture into the soup and cook
for 4 minutes, or until thickened.

Ladle the soup into warmed soup bowls,
garnish with chopped parsley, and serve
at once.

serves 4 | prep 10 minutes | cook 6–8 minutes

CORN & CRAB SOUP

2 tbsp vegetable or peanut oil
4 garlic cloves, finely chopped
5 shallots, finely chopped
2 lemon grass stalks, finely chopped
1-inch/2.5-cm piece fresh gingerroot,
  finely chopped
4 cups chicken stock
1³/₄ cups canned coconut milk
1³/₈ cups frozen corn kernels
12 oz/350 g canned crabmeat,
  drained and flaked
2 tbsp Thai fish sauce
juice of 1 lime
1 tsp jaggery or brown sugar
bunch of fresh cilantro, chopped,
  to garnish

Heat the oil in a large skillet over low heat, add the garlic, shallots, lemon grass, and ginger, and cook, stirring occasionally, for 2–3 minutes until softened. Add the stock and coconut milk and bring to a boil. Add the corn, reduce the heat, and let simmer gently for 3–4 minutes.

Add the crabmeat, fish sauce, lime juice, and sugar and let simmer gently for 1 minute. Ladle into warmed bowls, garnish with the chopped cilantro and serve at once.

serves 4 | prep 15 minutes | cook 40 minutes

HADDOCK & POTATO SOUP

Melt the butter in a large pan over medium heat, add the onion and leek, and cook, stirring frequently, for 3 minutes, or until slightly softened. Mix the flour in a bowl with enough of the milk to make a smooth paste, then stir into the pan. Cook, stirring constantly, for 2 minutes, then gradually stir in the remaining milk. Add the bay leaf and parsley and season to taste with salt and pepper. Bring to a boil, then reduce the heat and let simmer for 15 minutes.

Rinse the haddock fillets under cold running water, drain, then cut into bite-size chunks. Add to the soup and cook for 15 minutes, or until the fish is tender and cooked right through. Add the mashed potatoes and stir in the cream. Cook for an additional 2–3 minutes, then remove from the heat and remove and discard the bay leaf.

Ladle into warmed serving bowls, garnish with chopped parsley, and serve with crusty rolls and a green salad.

2 tbsp butter
1 onion, chopped
1 leek, chopped
2 tbsp all-purpose flour
3½ cups milk
1 bay leaf
2 tbsp chopped fresh parsley, plus
  extra to garnish
12 oz/350 g smoked haddock
  fillets, skinned
1 lb/450 g potatoes, cooked
  and mashed
6 tbsp heavy cream
salt and pepper

TO SERVE
crusty rolls
green salad

serves 4 | *prep* 10 minutes | *cook* 30 minutes

SMOKED COD CHOWDER

2 tbsp butter
1 onion, finely chopped
1 small celery stalk, finely diced
9 oz/250 g potatoes, diced
2 oz/55 g carrots, diced
1¼ cups boiling water
12 oz/350 g smoked cod fillets,
   skinned and cut into
   bite-size pieces
1¼ cups milk
salt and pepper

Melt the butter in a large pan over low heat, add the onion and celery, and cook, stirring frequently, for 5 minutes, or until softened but not browned.

Add the potatoes, carrots, water, and salt and pepper to taste. Bring to a boil, then reduce the heat and let simmer for 10 minutes, or until the vegetables are tender. Add the fish to the chowder and cook for an additional 10 minutes.

Pour in the milk and heat gently. Taste and adjust the seasoning, if necessary. Serve hot.

serves 4 | prep 20 minutes | cook 40–45 minutes

CARIBBEAN FISH CHOWDER

Heat the oil with the cumin seeds and thyme in a large pan over medium heat. Add the onion, bell pepper, sweet potato, chilies, and garlic and cook, stirring constantly, for 1 minute.

Reduce the heat to medium–low, cover, and cook for 10 minutes, or until beginning to soften.

Pour in the stock and season generously with salt and pepper. Bring to a boil, then reduce the heat to medium–low, cover, and let simmer for 20 minutes.

Add the snapper, peas, corn, and cream. Cook over low heat, uncovered and without boiling, for 7–10 minutes until the fish is just cooked.

Serve at once, garnished with cilantro.

3 tbsp vegetable oil
1 tsp cumin seeds, crushed
1 tsp dried thyme or oregano
1 onion, diced
1/2 green bell pepper, seeded and diced
1 sweet potato, diced
2–3 fresh green chilies, seeded and very finely chopped
1 garlic clove, very finely chopped
4 cups chicken stock
14 oz/400 g red snapper fillets, skinned and cut into chunks
1/4 cup frozen peas
1/4 cup frozen corn kernels
1/2 cup light cream
salt and pepper
3 tbsp chopped fresh cilantro, to garnish

serves 4 | *prep* 10 minutes | *cook* 8–10 minutes

SHRIMP LAKSA

Put the coconut milk and stock in a pan over medium heat and bring slowly to a boil. Add all the remaining ingredients, except the shrimp, reduce the heat to low, and let simmer gently for 4–5 minutes until the noodles are cooked.

Add the shrimp and let simmer for an additional 1–2 minutes until heated through. Ladle the soup into small warmed bowls, dividing the shrimp equally between them, and serve at once.

1¾ cups canned coconut milk
1¼ cups vegetable stock
1¾ oz/50 g dried vermicelli
   rice noodles
1 red bell pepper, seeded and cut
   into strips
8 oz/225 g canned bamboo shoots,
   drained and rinsed
2-inch/5-cm piece fresh gingerroot,
   thinly sliced
3 scallions, chopped
1 tbsp Thai Red Curry Paste
2 tbsp Thai fish sauce
1 tsp jaggery or brown sugar
6 fresh Thai basil sprigs
12 cooked shrimp, in their shells

serves 4 | prep 15 minutes | cook 45 minutes

SHRIMP GUMBO

Melt the butter with the oil in a large pan over medium heat, add the okra, and cook, uncovered and stirring frequently, for 15 minutes, or until the okra loses its gummy consistency.

Add the onion, celery, bell pepper, garlic, tomatoes, thyme, bay leaf, and salt and pepper to taste. Cover and cook over medium–low heat for 10 minutes.

Pour in the stock. Bring to a boil, then reduce the heat to medium–low, cover, and let simmer for 15 minutes, or until the vegetables are al dente. Add the shrimp and Tabasco sauce and cook for 5 minutes, or until the shrimp turn pink.

Stir in the cilantro to garnish and serve.

2 tbsp butter
2 tbsp vegetable oil
9 oz/250 g okra, trimmed and
  thickly sliced
1 onion, finely chopped
2 celery stalks, quartered lengthwise
  and diced
1 green bell pepper, seeded
  and diced
2 garlic cloves, very finely chopped
7 oz/200 g canned chopped tomatoes
1/2 tsp dried thyme or oregano
1 fresh bay leaf
3 1/2 pints chicken stock or water
1 lb/450 g fresh or frozen raw shrimp,
  shelled and deveined
few drops of Tabasco sauce
salt and pepper
2 tbsp chopped fresh cilantro,
  to garnish

serves 4 | *prep 25 minutes* | *cook 45 minutes*

BOUILLABAISSE

generous ⅓ cup olive oil
3 garlic cloves, chopped
1 onion, chopped
2 scallions, sliced
2 tomatoes, seeded and chopped
1 fennel bulb, chopped
3 cups fish stock
1¾ cups dry white wine
1 bay leaf
pinch of saffron threads
1 tbsp chopped fresh oregano
1 tbsp chopped fresh basil
2 tbsp chopped fresh parsley
7 oz/200 g live mussels
1 lb 2 oz/500 g snapper or
    angler fish fillets, skinned
7 oz/200 g cooked shrimp, shelled
    and deveined
salt and pepper
thick slices of French bread, to serve

Heat the oil in a large pan over medium heat, add the garlic, onion, and scallions, and cook, stirring frequently, for 3 minutes. Stir in the tomatoes, fennel, stock, wine, bay leaf, saffron, and herbs. Bring to a boil, then reduce the heat, cover, and let simmer for 30 minutes.

Meanwhile, clean the mussels by scrubbing or scraping the shells and pulling out any beards that are attached to them. Discard any with broken shells or any that refuse to close when tapped. Put the mussels in a colander and rinse well under cold running water. Put them in a large pan with just the water that clings to their shells and cook, covered, over high heat, shaking the pan occasionally, for 3–4 minutes, or until the mussels have opened. Discard any mussels that remain closed. Drain and set aside.

Rinse the snapper under cold running water, pat dry with paper towels, then cut into small chunks. Add to the tomato mixture and let simmer for 5 minutes. Add the mussels and shrimp, season to taste with salt and pepper, and cook for 5 minutes, or until the shrimp turn pink. Remove and discard the bay leaf and ladle the soup into warmed serving bowls. Serve with thick slices of French bread.

serves 4 | prep 25 minutes | cook 45 minutes

CIOPPINO

2 tbsp butter
3 tbsp olive oil
2 garlic cloves, chopped
1 onion, chopped
14 oz/400 g canned chopped
    tomatoes
2 cups fish stock
scant 1 cup dry white wine
1 bay leaf
1 tsp dried mixed herbs
7 oz/200 g live mussels
12 oz/350 g cod fillets, rinsed, dried,
    and cut into chunks
12 oz/350 g raw shrimp, shelled
    and deveined
7 oz/200 g cooked lobster meat, cut
    into chunks
salt and pepper
fresh flat-leaf parsley sprigs,
    to garnish
crusty bread, to serve

Melt the butter with the oil in a large pan
over medium heat, add the garlic and onion,
and cook, stirring, for 3 minutes. Stir in the
tomatoes, stock, wine, bay leaf, and herbs.
Bring to a boil, then reduce the heat, cover,
and let simmer for 30 minutes. Meanwhile,
clean the mussels by scrubbing or scraping
the shells and pulling out any beards that are
attached to them. Discard any with broken
shells or any that refuse to close when tapped.
Put the mussels in a colander and rinse well
under cold running water. Put them into a
large pan with just the water that clings to
their shells and cook, covered, over high heat,
shaking the pan occasionally, for 3–4 minutes,
or until the mussels have opened. Discard any
that remain closed. Drain and set aside.

Add the cod to the tomato mixture and simmer
for 3 minutes. Add the mussels and shrimp and
cook for 5 minutes, or until the shrimp turn
pink. Stir in the lobster, season to taste with
salt and pepper, and let simmer for 1 minute.
Remove and discard the bay leaf and ladle the
soup into warmed serving bowls. Garnish with
parsley sprigs and serve with crusty bread.

serves 4 | *prep 20 minutes* | *cook 25–30 minutes*

NEW ENGLAND CLAM CHOWDER

2 lb/900 g live clams
4 rindless lean bacon slices, chopped
2 tbsp butter
1 onion, chopped
1 tbsp chopped fresh thyme
1 large potato, diced
1¹/₄ cups milk
1 bay leaf
²/₃ cup heavy cream
1 tbsp chopped fresh parsley
salt and pepper

Scrub the clams and put in a large pan with a splash of water. Cook over high heat for 3–4 minutes until all the clams have opened. Discard any that remain closed. Drain the clams, reserving the cooking liquid. Set aside until cool enough to handle.

Set aside 8 clams in their shells to garnish. Remove the remaining clams from their shells, coarsely chop if large and set aside.

Heat a clean, dry pan over medium–high heat, add the bacon, and cook, stirring frequently, for 5 minutes, or until browned and crisp. Remove with a slotted spoon and drain on paper towels. Melt the butter in the pan, add the onion, and cook, stirring frequently, for 4–5 minutes until softened but not browned. Add the thyme and cook briefly before adding the potato, reserved clam cooking liquid, milk, and bay leaf. Bring to a boil, then reduce the heat and let simmer for 10 minutes, or until the potato is tender but not falling apart.

Let the soup cool slightly, then transfer to a blender or food processor and process until smooth.

Return the soup to the pan and add the shelled clams, bacon, and cream. Let simmer for an additional 2–3 minutes. Season to taste with salt and pepper and stir in the parsley. Ladle into warmed serving bowls, garnish with the reserved clams in their shells, and serve.

serves 4 | *prep* 15 minutes | *cook* 45–50 minutes

BASQUE TUNA STEW

5 tbsp olive oil
1 large onion, chopped
2 garlic cloves, chopped
7 oz/200 g canned chopped
  tomatoes
1 lb 9 oz/700 g potatoes, cut
  into 2-inch/5-cm chunks
3 green bell peppers, seeded and
  coarsely chopped
1¼ cups cold water
2 lb/900 g fresh tuna, cut into
  chunks
4 slices crusty white bread
salt and pepper

Heat 2 tablespoons of the oil in a pan over
medium heat, add the onion, and cook,
stirring frequently, for 8–10 minutes until
softened and browned. Add the garlic and
cook, stirring, for an additional minute.
Add the tomatoes, cover, and let simmer
for 30 minutes, or until thickened.

Meanwhile, in a separate pan, mix together
the potatoes and bell peppers. Add the water
(which should just cover the vegetables) and
bring to a boil, then reduce the heat and let
simmer for 15 minutes, or until the potatoes
are almost tender.

Add the tuna and the tomato mixture to the
potatoes and bell peppers and season to
taste with salt and pepper. Cover and simmer
for 6–8 minutes until the tuna is tender.

Meanwhile, heat the remaining oil in a large
skillet over medium heat, add the bread
slices, and cook on both sides until golden.
Remove with a slotted spoon and drain on
paper towels. Serve with the stew.

serves 4 | prep 25 minutes | cook 55 minutes

CHUNKY COD STEW
WITH CELERY & POTATOES

2 red bell peppers, halved and seeded
3 tbsp olive oil
1 onion, finely chopped
2 garlic cloves, very finely chopped
1 tbsp white wine vinegar
1 tbsp tomato paste
1 tbsp dried thyme or oregano
generous 1 cup fish stock
2 celery stalks, finely sliced
1 lb 5 oz/600 g fresh or frozen thick
  cod steaks, cut into chunks
1/2 cup stale coarse white
  bread crumbs
8–10 black olives, pitted and sliced
salt and pepper
chopped celery leaves, to garnish

Preheat the oven to 400°F/200°C. Cook the bell peppers, cut-side down, on a baking sheet under a preheated hot broiler for 10–12 minutes until beginning to blacken. Meanwhile, heat 1 tablespoon of the oil in an ovenproof casserole, add the onion, and cook, stirring frequently, for 5 minutes. Add the garlic, vinegar, tomato paste, and half the thyme. Cook, stirring, for 1 minute. Add the stock and let simmer for 5 minutes.

When cool enough to handle, peel the skin off the bell peppers. Coarsely chop the flesh. Put in a blender or food processor with the onion mixture and season to taste. Process until smooth. Pour into the casserole, add the celery and cod, and bring to a boil. Cover and bake in the oven for 35 minutes.

Combine the bread crumbs, remaining oil, olives, remaining thyme, and salt and pepper to taste in a small bowl. Sprinkle over the stew. Brown under a hot broiler for 5 minutes. Garnish with celery leaves before serving.

serves 4 | prep 15 minutes | cook 40 minutes

SPANISH SWORDFISH STEW

4 tbsp olive oil
3 shallots, chopped
2 garlic cloves, chopped
8 oz/225 g canned chopped tomatoes
1 tbsp tomato paste
1 lb 7 oz/650 g potatoes, sliced
generous 1 cup vegetable stock
2 tbsp lemon juice
1 red bell pepper, seeded and
    chopped
1 orange bell pepper, seeded
    and chopped
20 black olives, pitted and halved
2 lb 4 oz/1 kg swordfish steak,
    skinned and cut into
    bite-size pieces
salt and pepper
crusty bread, to serve

TO GARNISH
fresh flat-leaf parsley sprigs
lemon slices

Heat the oil in a pan over low heat, add the shallots, and cook, stirring frequently, for 4 minutes, or until softened. Add the garlic, tomatoes, and tomato paste, cover, and let simmer gently for 20 minutes.

Meanwhile, put the potatoes in an ovenproof casserole with the stock and lemon juice. Bring to a boil, then reduce the heat and add the bell peppers. Cover and cook for 15 minutes.

Add the olives, swordfish, and the tomato mixture to the potatoes. Season to taste with salt and pepper. Stir well, then cover and let simmer for 7–10 minutes, or until the swordfish is cooked to your taste.

Remove from the heat and garnish with parsley sprigs and lemon slices. Serve with crusty bread.

serves 6 | prep 20 minutes | cook 30 minutes

LOUISIANA GUMBO

Heat half the oil in a large, ovenproof casserole over low heat, add the okra, and cook, stirring frequently, for 5 minutes, or until browned. Remove with a slotted spoon and set aside. Heat the remaining oil in the casserole, add the onion and celery and cook, stirring frequently, for 5 minutes, or until softened. Add the garlic and cook, stirring, for 1 minute. Stir in the flour, sugar, cumin, and salt and pepper to taste. Cook, stirring, for 2 minutes, then gradually stir in the stock and bring to a boil, stirring constantly.

Return the reserved okra to the casserole and add the bell peppers and tomatoes. Partially cover, reduce the heat to very low, and let simmer gently, stirring occasionally, for 10 minutes. Shell and devein the shrimp and set aside.

Add the parsley, cilantro, and Tabasco sauce to the casserole, then gently stir in the fish and shrimp. Cover and let simmer gently for 5 minutes, or until the fish is cooked through and the shrimp turn pink. Transfer to a large, warmed serving dish and serve.

2 tbsp sunflower-seed or corn oil
6 oz/175 g okra, trimmed and cut into
    1-inch/2.5-cm pieces
2 onions, very finely chopped
4 celery stalks, very finely chopped
1 garlic clove, finely chopped
2 tbsp all-purpose flour
½ tsp sugar
1 tsp ground cumin
3 cups fish stock
1 red bell pepper, seeded and
    chopped
1 green bell pepper, seeded
    and chopped
2 large tomatoes
12 oz/350 g large raw shrimp
4 tbsp chopped fresh parsley
1 tbsp chopped fresh cilantro
dash of Tabasco sauce, or to taste
12 oz/350 g cod fillets, skinned and
    cut into 1-inch/2.5-cm cubes
12 oz/350 g angler fish fillets, cut
    into 1-inch/2.5-cm cubes
salt and pepper

serves 4–6 | prep 35 minutes | cook 30–35 minutes

CATALAN FISH STEW

large pinch of saffron threads
4 tbsp boiling water
6 tbsp olive oil
1 large onion, chopped
2 garlic cloves, finely chopped
1½ tbsp chopped fresh thyme leaves
2 bay leaves
2 red bell peppers, seeded and
    coarsely chopped
1 lb 12 oz/800 g canned chopped
    tomatoes
1 tsp smoked paprika
generous 1 cup fish stock
scant 1 cup blanched almonds,
    toasted and finely ground
1 lb 5 oz/600 g thick hake or cod
    fillets, skinned and cut into 2-inch/
    5-cm chunks
12–16 raw shrimp, shelled and
    deveined
12–16 live mussels, scrubbed and
    debearded
12–16 live clams, scrubbed
salt and pepper
thick crusty bread, to serve

Put the saffron threads in a heatproof bowl, add
the boiling water, and set aside to infuse.

Heat the oil in a large, heavy-bottom, ovenproof
casserole over medium–high heat. Reduce the heat
to low, add the onion, and cook, stirring
occasionally, for 10 minutes, or until golden
but not browned. Stir in the garlic, thyme, bay
leaves, and bell peppers and cook for 5 minutes,
or until the bell peppers are soft .

Add the tomatoes and paprika and let simmer,
stirring frequently, for 5 minutes.

Stir in the stock, reserved saffron water, and ground
almonds and bring to a boil, stirring frequently.
Reduce the heat and let simmer for 5–10 minutes
until the sauce reduces and thickens. Add salt and
pepper to taste.

Gently stir in the hake so that it doesn't break
up and add the shrimp, mussels, and clams. Reduce
the heat to very low, cover the casserole, and let
simmer for 5 minutes, or until the hake is cooked
through, the shrimp turn pink, and the mussels
and clams open. Discard any mussels or clams that
remain closed. Serve at once with plenty of thick,
crusty bread for soaking up the juices.

serves 4 | prep 30 minutes | cook 25 minutes

BRAZILIAN SEAFOOD STEW

2 tbsp olive oil
1 onion, finely chopped
2 garlic cloves, very finely chopped
14 oz/400 g canned
   chopped tomatoes
1/4 tsp cayenne pepper
pinch of saffron threads
2 lb/900 g cod steaks, cut into chunks
1 lb/450 g mussels, scrubbed
   and debearded
8 oz/225 g raw jumbo shrimp, shelled
   and deveined
7 oz/200 g canned crabmeat, drained
7 oz/200 g bottled clams
salt and pepper
3 tbsp chopped fresh cilantro,
   to garnish

Heat the oil in a large pan or ovenproof casserole over medium heat, add the onion, and cook, stirring frequently, for 5 minutes, or until softened.

Stir in the garlic, tomatoes, cayenne pepper, and saffron. Season to taste with salt and pepper and let simmer, stirring occasionally, for 5 minutes.

Add the cod and mussels, then pour in enough water to just cover and bring to a boil. Reduce the heat to low, cover, and let simmer for 10 minutes, or until the mussels have opened. Discard any that remain closed.

Add the shrimp, crabmeat, and clams with their juice. Let simmer for an additional 5 minutes, or until the shrimp turn pink.

Stir in the cilantro just before serving.

5

Enjoy fish at its laid-back, comforting best in this selection of classic dishes. Here it is combined with eggs, simmered with rice, tossed with pasta and noodles, or encased in rich, crumbling pie dough or a crisp bread crumb or batter coating. It is even wrapped up in a warm tortilla for good measure.

LIGHT LUNCHES AND SUPPER DISHES

While fresh fish features in many of the recipes—including smoked fish, which works so well with cheese and spices—several dishes use pantry or freezer ingredients for convenience. Canned anchovies, for instance, along with bottled olives and capers, make a gutsy impromptu pasta sauce, and frozen shrimp and canned tuna combine to create a tasty seafood omelet.

serves 4 | prep 10 minutes | cook 30 minutes

KEDGEREE

1 lb/450 g undyed smoked haddock,
  skinned
2 tbsp olive oil
1 onion, finely chopped
1 tsp mild curry paste
generous 3/4 cup long-grain white rice
4 tbsp butter
3 hard-cooked eggs
salt and pepper
2 tbsp chopped fresh parsley,
  to garnish

Put the fish in a large pan and cover with water. Bring the water to a boil, then reduce the heat and let simmer for 8–10 minutes until the fish flakes easily.

Remove the fish with a slotted spoon and keep warm, reserving the cooking liquid in a pitcher or bowl.

Heat the oil in the pan over medium heat, add the onion, and cook, stirring frequently, for 4 minutes, or until softened. Stir in the curry paste and add the rice.

Measure 2 1/2 cups of the haddock cooking liquid and return to the pan. Bring to a simmer and cover. Cook for 10–12 minutes until the rice is tender and the water has been absorbed. Season to taste with salt and pepper.

Flake the fish and add to the pan with the butter. Stir very gently over low heat until the butter has melted. Chop 2 of the hard-cooked eggs and add to the pan.

Turn the kedgeree into a serving dish, slice the remaining egg, and use to garnish. Sprinkle over the chopped parsley and serve at once.

serves 6 | prep 25 minutes, plus 40 minutes' chilling and resting | cook 30 minutes

SMOKED HADDOCK & GRUYERE SOUFFLE TART

PIE DOUGH
scant 1 cup all-purpose flour, plus extra for dusting
pinch of salt
4 tbsp cold butter, diced, plus extra for greasing
1/2 tsp English mustard powder
1 egg yolk

FILLING
1 1/4 cups milk
1 bay leaf
9 oz/250 g undyed smoked haddock
2 tbsp butter
scant 1/4 cup all-purpose flour
1/2 tsp ground nutmeg
4 1/2 oz/125 g Gruyère cheese, grated
2 eggs, separated
white pepper

Lightly grease a 9-inch/23-cm loose-bottom fluted tart pan. Sift the flour with the salt into a food processor, add the butter, and process until the mixture resembles fine bread crumbs. Tip the mixture into a large bowl and sprinkle in the mustard powder. Mix the egg yolk with a little cold water and add a little of the mixture to the bowl, just enough to bring the dough together. Turn out onto a lightly floured counter and roll out the dough to a circle 3 1/4 inches/8 cm wider in diameter than the pan. Line the pan with the dough and trim the edge. Line the tart shell with parchment paper and fill with dried beans. Let chill in the refrigerator for 30 minutes. Meanwhile, preheat the oven to 375°F/190°C.

Remove the tart shell from the refrigerator and bake in the preheated oven for 10 minutes. Remove the paper and beans and bake the tart shell for another 5 minutes.

Meanwhile, put the milk and bay leaf in a skillet and bring to a simmer. Add the

haddock and cook for 3–5 minutes until just cooked. Remove and discard the bay leaf and carefully remove the fish with a slotted spoon, reserving the milk. When cool enough to handle, flake the fish, removing and discarding any bones or skin. Increase the oven temperature to 400°F/200°C.

Melt the butter in a pan, stir in the flour, and cook, stirring constantly, for 2–3 minutes. Gradually add the reserved cooking milk and cook, stirring constantly, for another 5 minutes, or until thickened. Stir in the nutmeg and pepper to taste, then the cheese. Remove the sauce from the heat, stir in the egg yolks and fish, and let cool slightly. Meanwhile, whisk the egg whites in a clean, greasefree bowl until stiff, then fold quickly and lightly into the fish mixture. Immediately pour into the tart shell and bake for 15 minutes until puffed up and browned. Remove the tart from the oven, let rest for 10 minutes, then serve.

serves 2 | prep 10 minutes | cook 20 minutes

OMELET ARNOLD BENNETT

6 oz/175 g undyed smoked haddock,
   skinned
2 tbsp butter
4 eggs
1 tbsp olive oil
4 tbsp light cream
2 tbsp grated Cheddar or
   Parmesan cheese
salt and pepper

Put the haddock in a large pan and cover with water. Bring the water to a boil, then reduce the heat and let simmer for 8–10 minutes until the fish flakes easily. Remove the fish with a slotted spoon and drain onto a plate. When cool enough to handle, flake the fish, removing and discarding any bones.

Melt half the butter in a small pan and add the haddock to warm.

In a bowl, beat the eggs together gently with a fork and season to taste with salt and pepper, taking care not to add too much salt because the haddock will be quite salty.

Melt the remaining butter with the oil in a 9-inch/23-cm skillet with a heatproof handle over medium heat. When the butter starts to froth, pour in the eggs and spread them around by tilting the skillet. Use a spatula or fork to move the egg around until it is cooked underneath but still liquid on top.

Tip in the warm haddock and spread over the omelet.

Pour over the cream and top with the cheese, then place the skillet under a preheated hot broiler for 1 minute until the cheese is melted. Serve at once on warmed plates.

serves 4 | *prep* 30 minutes, plus 30 minutes' chilling | *cook* 15–20 minutes

HADDOCK GOUJONS

6 oz/175 g herb focaccia bread
1 lb 9 oz/700 g skinless, boneless
  haddock fillet
2–3 tbsp all-purpose flour
2 eggs, lightly beaten
vegetable oil, for deep-frying
fresh parsley sprigs, to garnish
lemon wedges, to serve

TARTARE SAUCE
1 egg yolk
1 tsp Dijon mustard
2 tsp white wine vinegar
²/₃ cup light olive oil
1 tsp finely chopped green olives
1 tsp finely chopped gherkins
1 tsp finely chopped capers
2 tsp snipped fresh chives
2 tsp chopped fresh parsley
salt and pepper

Put the focaccia in a food processor and process to fine bread crumbs. Set aside. Thinly slice the haddock fillet widthwise into fingers. Put the flour, egg, and bread crumbs in separate bowls.

Dip the haddock fingers into the flour, then the egg and finally the bread crumbs to coat. Lay on a plate, cover, and let chill in the refrigerator for 30 minutes. To make the tartare sauce, put the egg yolk, mustard, vinegar, and salt and pepper to taste in a blender or clean food processor. Process for 30 seconds until frothy. Begin adding the olive oil through the feed tube, drop by drop, until the mixture begins to thicken. Continue adding the oil in a slow, steady stream until all the oil is incorporated.

Transfer to a small bowl and stir in the remaining ingredients. Check and adjust the seasoning, if necessary. Add a little hot water if the sauce is too thick.

Heat the vegetable oil in deep-fat fryer, large, heavy-bottom pan, or wok to 350–375°F/ 180–190°C, or until a cube of bread browns in 30 seconds. Deep-fry 3–4 goujons at a time for 3–4 minutes until the crumbs are browned and crisp and the fish is cooked. Remove with a slotted spoon and drain on paper towels. Keep warm while you cook the remaining fish.

Serve the goujons at once, with tartare sauce and lemon wedges for squeezing over.

serves 6 | *prep 20 minutes* | *cook 40 minutes*

SALMON FRITTATA

9 oz/250 g skinless, boneless salmon
3 fresh thyme sprigs
1 fresh parsley sprig plus 2 tbsp
  chopped fresh parsley
5 black peppercorns
1/2 small onion, sliced
1/2 celery stalk, sliced
1/2 carrot, chopped
6 oz/175 g asparagus spears, chopped
3 oz/85 g baby carrots, halved
31/2 tbsp butter
1 large onion, finely sliced
1 garlic clove, finely chopped
1 cup fresh or frozen peas
8 eggs, lightly beaten
1 tbsp chopped fresh dill
salt and pepper
lemon wedges, to garnish

TO SERVE
sour cream
salad
crusty bread

Put the salmon in a pan with 1 thyme sprig, the parsley sprig, peppercorns, onion, celery, and carrot. Cover the vegetables and fish with cold water and bring slowly to a boil. Remove the pan from the heat and let stand for 5 minutes. Remove the fish with a slotted spoon, flake, and set aside. Discard the vegetables and cooking liquid.

Bring a large pan of salted water to a boil and blanch the asparagus for 2 minutes. Drain and refresh under cold running water. Blanch the baby carrots for 4 minutes. Drain and refresh under cold running water. Drain both again and pat dry. Set aside.

Heat half the butter in a large skillet with an ovenproof handle over medium–low heat, add the onion, and cook, stirring occasionally, for 8–10 minutes until softened but not browned. Add the garlic and remaining thyme and cook, stirring, for an additional minute. Add the asparagus, carrot, and peas and heat through.

Transfer to the eggs in a bowl with the chopped parsley, dill, salmon, and salt and pepper to taste. Stir briefly. Heat the remaining butter in the pan over low heat and return the mixture to the pan. Cover and cook for 10 minutes.

Cook under a preheated medium broiler for an additional 5 minutes until set and golden. Serve hot or cold in wedges, topped with a spoonful of sour cream, with salad and crusty bread. Garnish with lemon wedges.

serves 3 | *prep 20 minutes* | *cook 25 minutes*

SEAFOOD OMELET

2 tbsp unsalted butter
1 tbsp olive oil
1 onion, very finely chopped
6 oz/175 g zucchini, halved lengthwise
  and sliced
1 celery stalk, very finely chopped
3 oz/85 g white mushrooms, sliced
2 oz/55 g green beans, cut into
  2-inch/5-cm lengths
4 eggs
3/8 cup mascarpone cheese
1 tbsp chopped fresh thyme
1 tbsp shredded fresh basil
7 oz/200 g canned tuna, drained
  and flaked
4 oz/115 g cooked shelled shrimp,
  thawed if frozen
salt and pepper

Melt the butter with the oil in a heavy-bottom skillet with an ovenproof handle over low heat. Add the onion and cook, stirring occasionally, for 5 minutes until softened.

Add the zucchini, celery, mushrooms, and beans and cook, stirring occasionally, for another 8–10 minutes until starting to brown.

Beat the eggs with the cheese, thyme, basil, and salt and pepper to taste in a bowl.

Add the tuna to the skillet and stir it into the mixture with a wooden spoon, then stir in the shrimp.

Pour the egg mixture into the skillet and cook for 5 minutes, or until it is just beginning to set. Draw the egg from the sides of the skillet toward the center to allow the uncooked egg to run underneath.

Put the skillet under a preheated hot broiler and cook until the egg is set and the surface is beginning to brown. Cut the omelet into wedges and serve.

serves 4 | *prep* 15 minutes, plus 5 hours' chilling | *cook* 12 minutes

PAN BAGNA

16-inch/40-cm country-style loaf,
    thicker than a French baguette
fruity extra virgin olive oil
ready-made tapenade (optional)

FILLING
2 eggs
1³/₄ oz/50 g canned anchovy fillets
    in oil
about 3 oz/85 g herb-, garlic- or chili-
    flavored olives
lettuce or arugula leaves, rinsed and
    patted dry
about 4 plum tomatoes, sliced
7 oz/200 g canned tuna in brine, well
    drained and flaked

Bring a pan of water to a boil, add the eggs and return to a boil. Boil for 12 minutes. Drain and immediately plunge into a bowl of ice-cold water to prevent further cooking.

Shell the cooked eggs and cut into slices. Drain the anchovy fillets well, then cut them in half lengthwise if large. Pit the olives and halve. Set aside.

Using a serrated knife, slice the loaf horizontally in half. Remove about ¹/₂ inch/ 1 cm of the crumb from the top and bottom, leaving a border all around both halves.

Generously brush both halves with the oil. Spread with tapenade, if you like a strong, robust flavor. Arrange a layer of lettuce leaves on the bottom half.

Add layers of hard-cooked egg slices, tomato slices, olives, anchovies, and tuna, sprinkling with oil and adding lettuce leaves between the layers. Make the filling as thick as you like.

Place the other bread half on top and press down firmly. Wrap tightly in plastic wrap and put on a board or plate that will fit in your refrigerator. Weight down with food cans and let chill in the refrigerator for several hours. To serve, slice into 4 equal portions, tying with string to secure in place, if wished.

serves 4 | prep 20 minutes, plus 30 minutes' chilling | cook 30–35 minutes

FISH CAKES

1 lb/450 g mealy potatoes, such as
Russet Burbank, Russet Arcadia, or
Butte, peeled and cut into chunks
1 lb/450 g mixed fish fillets, such as
cod and salmon, skinned
2 tbsp chopped fresh tarragon
grated rind of 1 lemon
2 tbsp heavy cream
1 tbsp all-purpose flour
1 egg, beaten
1 cup bread crumbs, made from day-
old white or whole wheat bread
4 tbsp vegetable oil
salt and pepper
lemon wedges, to garnish
watercress salad, to serve

Bring a large pan of salted water to a boil, add the potatoes, and cook for 15–20 minutes. Drain well, then mash with a potato masher or fork until smooth.

Put the fish in a skillet and just cover with water. Bring to a boil over medium heat, then reduce the heat to low, cover, and let simmer gently for 5 minutes until cooked.

Remove with a slotted spoon and drain on a plate. When cool enough to handle, flake the fish coarsely into good-size pieces, removing and discarding any bones.

Mix the mashed potatoes with the fish, tarragon, lemon rind, and cream in a bowl. Season well with salt and pepper and shape into 4 round cakes or 8 smaller ones with your hands.

Put the flour, egg, and bread crumbs in separate bowls. Dust the fish cakes with flour, dip into the beaten egg, then coat thoroughly in the bread crumbs. Put on a baking sheet, cover, and let chill in the refrigerator for at least 30 minutes.

Heat the oil in the skillet over medium heat, add the fish cakes, and cook for 5 minutes on each side, turning them with a spatula.

Garnish with lemon wedges and serve hot with a watercress salad.

serves 4 | prep 25 minutes, plus 30 minutes' resting | cook 20 minutes

DEEP-FRIED SEAFOOD

corn oil, for deep-frying
7 oz/200 g white fish fillets, such as
  English sole, skinned and cut
  into strips
7 oz/200 g angler fish fillets, cut into
  bite-size chunks
4 live scallops, shucked and cleaned
8 oz/225 g large cooked shrimp,
  shelled and deveined but
  with tails left intact

BATTER
generous ¾ cup all-purpose flour
pinch of salt
1 egg yolk
1 tbsp olive oil
1 cup milk
2 egg whites

TO GARNISH
fresh flat-leaf parsley sprigs
lemon wedges

First, make the batter. Sift the flour with the salt into a bowl and make a well in the center. Add the egg yolk and olive oil to the well and mix together with a wooden spoon, gradually incorporating the flour. Gradually beat in the milk to make a smooth batter. Cover and let rest for 30 minutes.

Heat the corn oil in a deep-fat fryer, large, heavy-bottom pan, or wok to 350–375°F/180–190°C, or until a cube of bread browns in 30 seconds.

Meanwhile, whisk the egg whites in a separate clean, greasefree bowl until they form stiff peaks. Gently fold into the batter.

Using tongs, dip the seafood, a piece at a time, into the batter to coat. Deep-fry in small batches for 3–4 minutes until crisp and golden (if you deep-fry too many pieces at a time, the oil temperature will drop and the batter will be soggy). Remove with a slotted spoon and drain on paper towels. Transfer to a warmed serving plate and keep warm in a low oven while you cook the remaining pieces.

Garnish with parsley sprigs and lemon wedges and serve.

serves 4 | prep 15 minutes | cook 20–25 minutes

FISH TACOS

¼ red cabbage, thinly sliced
  or shredded
¼ tsp dried oregano
¼ tsp ground cumin
1 tsp mild chili powder
2 garlic cloves, finely chopped
juice of 2 limes
hot pepper sauce or salsa, to taste
about 1 lb/450 g firm-fleshed white
  fish fillets, such as red snapper or
  cod, skinned and cut into chunks
3 tbsp all-purpose flour
vegetable oil, for frying
8 corn tortillas
1 tbsp chopped fresh cilantro
½ onion, chopped (optional)
salsa of your choice
salt and pepper

Combine the cabbage with half the oregano, cumin, chili powder, and garlic, then stir in the lime juice and salt and hot pepper sauce to taste. Set aside.

Put the fish on a plate and sprinkle with the remaining oregano, cumin, chili powder, and garlic and salt and pepper to taste. Dust with the flour.

Heat the oil in a skillet over high heat until it is smoking, add the fish and cook, turning frequently, in small batches until golden on the outside and just tender in the center. Remove with a slotted spoon and drain on paper towels. Keep warm in a low oven while you cook the remaining fish.

Heat the tortillas one by one in a dry nonstick skillet over medium heat, sprinkling with a few drops of water as they heat; wrap the tortillas in a clean dish towel as you work to keep them warm. Alternatively, heat through in a stack in the pan, alternating the tortillas from the top to the bottom to warm evenly.

Put some of the warm fried fish in each tortilla, along with a large spoonful of the cabbage salad. Sprinkle with chopped fresh cilantro and onion, if desired. Add the salsa to taste and serve at once.

serves 4 | prep 15 minutes, plus 15 minutes' cooling | cook 15–20 minutes

FISH & REFRIED BEAN TOSTADAS

about 1 lb/450 g firm-fleshed white fish
   fillets, such as red snapper or cod,
   skinned
1/2 cup fish stock
1/4 tsp ground cumin
1/4 tsp mild chili powder
pinch of dried oregano
4 garlic cloves, finely chopped
juice of 1/2 lemon or lime
8 soft corn tortillas
vegetable oil, for cooking
14 oz/400 g canned refried beans,
   warmed with 2 tbsp water to thin
salsa of your choice
2–3 romaine lettuce leaves, shredded
3 tbsp chopped fresh cilantro
2 tbsp chopped onion
salt and pepper

TO GARNISH
sour cream
chopped fresh herbs

Put the fish in a pan with the stock, cumin, chili powder, oregano, garlic, and salt and pepper to taste. Bring to a boil over medium heat, then immediately remove from the heat and let the fish cool in the cooking liquid.

When cool enough to handle, remove the fish with a slotted spoon, reserving the cooking liquid. Flake the fish into bite-size pieces and put in a nonmetallic bowl. Sprinkle with the lemon juice and set aside.

Heat a little oil in a nonstick skillet over high heat, add a tortilla, and cook on both sides until crisp. Drain on paper towels and keep warm while you cook the remainder. Spread the tostadas with the warm refried beans.

Gently reheat the fish with a little of the reserved fish cooking liquid in a pan. Spoon on top of the beans. Top each tostada with some salsa, lettuce, cilantro, and onion. Garnish each with a spoonful of sour cream and a sprinkling of herbs. Serve at once.

serves 4–6 | prep 10 minutes, plus 30 minutes' cooling | cook 10 minutes

FISH BURRITOS

about 1 lb/450 g firm-fleshed white
   fish fillets, such as red snapper
   or cod, skinned
¼ tsp ground cumin
pinch of dried oregano
4 garlic cloves, finely chopped
½ cup fish stock
juice of ½ lemon or lime
8 flour tortillas
2–3 romaine lettuce leaves, shredded
2 ripe tomatoes, diced
salsa of your choice
salt and pepper
lemon slices, to garnish

Season the fish to taste with salt and pepper,
then put in a pan with the cumin, oregano,
garlic, and enough stock to cover.

Bring to a boil and boil for 1 minute. Remove
the pan from the heat and let the fish cool in
the cooking liquid for about 30 minutes.

Remove the fish with a slotted spoon. Flake
the fish into bite-size pieces and put in a
nonmetallic bowl. Sprinkle with the lemon
juice and set aside.

Heat the tortillas in a dry nonstick skillet over
medium heat, sprinkling with a few drops of
water as they heat; wrap in a clean dish towel
as you work to keep them warm. Alternatively,
heat through in a stack in the pan, alternating
the tortillas from the top to the bottom to
warm evenly.

Arrange some lettuce in the center of
1 tortilla, spoon on a few fish chunks, then
sprinkle with a little tomato. Top with some
salsa. Repeat with the other tortillas and
serve at once, garnished with lemon slices.

serves 4 | *prep* 15 minutes, plus 30 minutes' chilling | *cook* 15 minutes

FISH & YOGURT QUENELLES

1 lb 10 oz/750 g white fish fillets, such
  as cod, pollock, or whiting, skinned
2 small egg whites
1/2 tsp ground coriander
1 tsp ground mace
2/3 cup lowfat plain yogurt
1 small onion, sliced
salt and pepper
mixed boiled basmati and wild rice,
  to serve

SAUCE
1 bunch of watercress
1 1/4 cups chicken stock
2 tbsp cornstarch
2/3 cup lowfat plain yogurt
2 tbsp low-fat sour cream

Cut the fish into pieces, put in a food
processor, and process for about 30 seconds.
Add the egg whites and process for another
30 seconds until the mixture forms a stiff
paste. Add the coriander, mace, yogurt, and
salt and pepper to taste and process until
smooth. Transfer to a bowl, cover, and chill
in the refrigerator for at least 30 minutes.

Spoon the mixture into a pastry bag and
pipe into sausage shapes about 4 inches/
10 cm long. Alternatively, take rounded
dessertspoons of the mixture and shape
into ovals using 2 spoons.

Bring about 2 inches/5 cm of water to a boil
in a skillet and add the onion. Using a spatula
or spoon, lower the quenelles into the water.
Cover and gently boil the quenelles
for 8 minutes, turning once. Remove with
a slotted spoon and drain.

To make the sauce, coarsely chop the
watercress, reserving a few sprigs for
garnishing. Put into a blender or food
processor with the stock and process until
well blended. Pour into a small pan. Stir
the cornstarch into the yogurt and pour
the mixture into the pan. Bring to a boil,
stirring constantly.

Stir in the sour cream and salt and pepper
to taste, then remove from the heat. Garnish
with the watercress sprigs. Serve with rice.

serves 4 | *prep* 10 minutes | *cook* 20–30 minutes

FRESH SARDINES BAKED
WITH LEMON & OREGANO

2 lemons, plus extra lemon wedges,
  to garnish
12 large fresh sardines, cleaned
4 tbsp olive oil
4 tbsp chopped fresh oregano
salt and pepper

Preheat the oven to 375°F/190°C. Slice 1 of the lemons and grate the rind and squeeze the juice from the second lemon.

Cut the heads off the sardines. Put the fish in a shallow, ovenproof dish large enough to hold them in a single layer. Put the lemon slices between the fish. Drizzle the lemon juice and oil over the fish. Sprinkle over the lemon rind and oregano and season to taste with salt and pepper.

Bake in the preheated oven for 20–30 minutes until the fish are tender. Serve garnished with lemon wedges.

serves 6–8 | prep 20 minutes, plus 1 hour 40 minutes' chilling and resting | cook 1 hour 40 minutes

PISSALADIERE

about 6 tbsp olive oil
3 large garlic cloves, crushed
2 lb 4 oz/1 kg onions, thinly sliced
3–4 tbsp ready-made tapenade
1³/₄ oz/50 g canned anchovy fillets in
  oil, drained and halved lengthwise
12 black olives, pitted
finely chopped fresh flat-leaf parsley,
  to garnish

PIE DOUGH
scant 1¹/₂ cups all-purpose flour
pinch of salt
6 tbsp butter, diced
2–3 tbsp ice-cold water

To make the pie dough, sift the flour with the salt into a bowl. Rub the butter into the flour until fine crumbs form. Mix in 2 tablespoons of the water to make a dough. Only add the extra water if necessary. Lightly knead the dough, then shape into a ball, wrap in plastic wrap, and let chill in the refrigerator for at least 1 hour.

Heat the oil in a large skillet with a tight-fitting lid over medium heat, add the garlic, and cook, stirring, for 2 minutes. Add the onions and stir to coat in oil. Reduce the heat to its lowest setting.

Dip a piece of parchment paper, large enough to fit over the top of the pan, in water. Shake off the excess and press it onto the onions. Cover with the lid and cook for 45 minutes, or until tender.

Meanwhile, roll out the dough on a lightly floured counter and use to line an 8-inch/20-cm loose-bottom tart pan. Prick all over with a fork, line with parchment paper, and fill with dried beans. Let chill in the refrigerator for 30 minutes. Preheat the oven to 425°F/220°C.

Put the pastry shell on a preheated baking shell and bake for 15 minutes. Remove the paper and beans and bake for an additional 5 minutes. Reduce the oven temperature to 350°F/180°C.

Spread the tapenade over the baked pastry shell, then fill with the onions. Arrange the anchovy fillets in a lattice pattern and sprinkle over the olives.

Bake for 25–30 minutes. Rest for 10 minutes. Remove from the pan, sprinkle with parsley, and serve.

serves 4 | *prep* 10 minutes | *cook* 30 minutes

LINGUINE WITH ANCHOVIES, OLIVES & CAPERS

3 tbsp olive oil
2 garlic cloves, finely chopped
10 canned anchovy fillets in oil,
  drained and chopped
generous ¾ cup black olives, pitted
  and chopped
1 tbsp capers, rinsed
1 lb/450 g plum tomatoes, peeled,
  seeded, and chopped
pinch of cayenne pepper
14 oz/400 g dried linguine
salt
2 tbsp chopped fresh flat-leaf parsley,
  to garnish

Heat the oil in a heavy-bottom pan over low heat, add the garlic, and cook, stirring frequently, for 2 minutes. Add the anchovies and mash them to a pulp with a fork. Add the olives, capers, and tomatoes and season to taste with cayenne pepper. Cover and let simmer for 25 minutes.

Meanwhile, bring a pan of lightly salted water to a boil. Add the pasta, return to a boil, and cook for 8–10 minutes until tender but still firm to the bite. Drain the pasta and transfer to a warmed serving dish.

Spoon the anchovy sauce into the dish and toss the pasta using 2 large forks. Garnish with chopped parsley and serve at once.

serves 6 | prep 15 minutes | cook 15 minutes

CREAMY SMOKED TROUT TAGLIATELLE

2 carrots, cut into thin sticks
2 celery stalks, cut into thin sticks
1 zucchini, cut into thin sticks
1 leek, cut into thin sticks
1 cup fresh or frozen peas
²/₃ cup vegetable stock
8 oz/225 g smoked trout fillets,
   skinned and cut into thin strips
⁷/₈ cup cream cheese
²/₃ cup dry white wine
2 tbsp chopped fresh dill, plus extra
   sprigs to garnish
8 oz/225 g dried tagliatelle
salt and pepper

Put the carrots, celery, zucchini, leek, and peas in a large, heavy-bottom pan and pour in the stock. Bring to a boil, then reduce the heat and let simmer for 5 minutes, or until the vegetables are tender and most of the stock has evaporated. Remove the pan from the heat, stir in the smoked trout, and cover to keep warm.

Put the cheese and wine in a separate large, heavy-bottom pan over low heat and stir until the cheese has melted and the mixture is smooth. Stir in the chopped dill and season to taste with salt and pepper.

Meanwhile, bring another large, heavy-bottom pan of lightly salted water to a boil. Add the pasta, return to a boil, and cook for 8–10 minutes until tender but still firm to the bite. Drain the pasta and tip into the cheese sauce. Toss the pasta using 2 large forks, then transfer to a warmed serving dish. Top with the smoked trout mixture, garnish with dill sprigs, and serve at once.

serves 4 | *prep* 15 minutes, plus 20 minutes' soaking | *cook* 10 minutes

SINGAPORE NOODLES

7 oz/200 g dried rice vermicelli
    noodles
1 tbsp mild, medium, or hot curry
    paste, to taste
1 tsp ground turmeric
6 tbsp water
2 tbsp peanut or sunflower-seed oil
1/2 onion, very thinly sliced
2 large garlic cloves, thinly sliced
3 oz/85 g broccoli, cut into
    very small florets
3 oz/85 g green beans, cut into
    1-inch/2.5-cm pieces
3 oz/85 g pork fillet, cut in half
    lengthwise and then into thin strips,
    or skinless, boneless chicken breast,
    thinly sliced
3 oz/85 g small cooked shelled
    shrimp, thawed if frozen
2 oz/55 g Napa cabbage or romaine
    lettuce, thinly shredded
1/4 fresh Thai chili, or to taste, seeded
    and thinly sliced
2 scallions, light green parts only,
    thinly shredded
fresh cilantro, to garnish

Soak the noodles in enough lukewarm water to cover in a bowl for 20 minutes, or until soft. Alternatively, cook according to the package instructions. Drain and set aside until required. Meanwhile, put the curry paste and turmeric in a small bowl and stir in 4 tablespoons of the water, then set aside.

Heat a wok or large skillet over high heat, add the oil, and heat until it simmers. Add the onion and garlic and stir-fry for 1 minute, or until softened. Add the broccoli and beans to the wok with the remaining water and stir-fry for an additional 2 minutes. Add the pork and stir-fry for 1 minute. Add the shrimp, Napa cabbage, and chili to the wok and stir-fry for an additional 2 minutes, or until the meat is cooked through and the vegetables are tender but still have a little bite. Remove with a slotted spoon and keep warm.

Add the scallions, noodles, and curry paste mixture to the wok. Mix the noodles and onions together using 2 forks and stir-fry for an additional 2 minutes, or until the noodles are hot and have picked up a dark golden color from the turmeric. Return the other ingredients to the wok and continue stir-frying and mixing for another minute. Serve at once, garnished with fresh cilantro.

serves 4 | *prep* 15 minutes, plus 20 minutes' soaking | *cook* 10 minutes

PAD THAI

7 oz/200 g dried medium or thick rice
  noodles
2 tbsp brown sugar
1 tbsp tamarind paste or 2 tbsp
  lemon juice
1 tbsp hot water
4 tbsp salted peanuts
1 tbsp peanut or sunflower-seed oil
1 shallot, finely chopped
10½ oz/300 g small cooked shelled
  shrimp, thawed if frozen
2 large eggs, beaten
2 oz/55 g firm tofu (drained weight),
  crumbled
2 tbsp Thai fish sauce
1 scallion, finely chopped
⅓ cup bean sprouts
large pinch of white sugar
pinch of dried red pepper flakes
chopped fresh cilantro, to garnish

Soak the noodles in enough lukewarm water
to cover in a bowl for 20 minutes, or until soft.
Alternatively, cook according to the package
instructions. Drain well and set aside.
Meanwhile, mix the brown sugar, tamarind paste,
and hot water together in a separate bowl,
stirring until the tamarind dissolves. Set aside.

Heat a wok or large skillet over high heat, add
the peanuts, and dry-fry, stirring constantly, until
they just turn golden. Immediately tip the
peanuts out of the wok, then finely chop and
set aside.

When you are ready to start cooking, reheat the
wok over high heat, add the oil, and heat until it
shimmers. Add the shallot and stir-fry for
30 seconds–1 minute until it starts to color.
Add the shrimp and stir-fry for an additional
30 seconds. Reduce the heat to medium. Push
the shallot and shrimp to one side of the wok,
pour the eggs into the wok, and stir-fry until
they are scrambled and firmly set. (You don't
want softly scrambled breakfast eggs for this.)

Return the heat to high, add the tofu to the pan,
and stir-fry to color. Add the noodles, tamarind
mixture, fish sauce, scallion, bean sprouts, white
sugar, and red pepper flakes. Mix all the
ingredients together using 2 large forks and
stir-fry for another 2 minutes to warm through.
Serve at once, sprinkled with cilantro.

serves 2 | prep 15 minutes, plus 10 minutes' standing | cook 20–25 minutes

SEAFOOD PIZZA

1 package pizza dough mix, about
    5 oz/140 g
all-purpose flour, for dusting
extra virgin olive oil, for oiling
    and drizzling
3–4 tbsp readymade tomato
    pizza sauce
8 oz/225 g mixed fresh seafood,
    including shrimp, mussels, and
    squid rings
1/2 red bell pepper, seeded and
    chopped
1/2 yellow bell pepper, seeded and
    chopped
1 tbsp capers, rinsed
2 oz/55 g Taleggio cheese, grated
3 tbsp freshly grated Parmesan
    cheese
1/2 tsp dried oregano
23/4 oz/75 g anchovy fillets in oil,
    drained and sliced
10 black olives, pitted
salt and pepper

Preheat the oven to 425°F/220°C. Prepare the pizza dough according to the package instructions. Turn out onto a lightly floured counter and knead for 5 minutes until smooth. Roll out the dough into an 8-inch/20-cm circle. Transfer to a lightly oiled baking sheet and push up the edge with your fingers to form a small rim. Let stand in a warm place for 10 minutes.

Spread the tomato sauce over the pizza base, almost to the edge. Arrange the mixed seafood, bell peppers, and capers on top.

Sprinkle the cheeses and oregano evenly over the topping. Add the anchovy fillets and olives, drizzle with oil, and season to taste with salt and pepper.

Bake in the preheated oven for 20–25 minutes until the crust is crisp and the cheese has melted. Serve at once.

serves 4 | prep 15 minutes | cook 25 minutes

SPAGHETTI WITH CLAMS

2 lb 4 oz/1 kg live clams
3/4 cup water
3/4 cup dry white wine
12 oz/350 g dried spaghetti
5 tbsp olive oil
2 garlic cloves, finely chopped
4 tbsp chopped fresh flat-leaf parsley
salt and pepper

Scrub the clams under cold running water. Discard any with broken shells or any that refuse to close when tapped. Put the clams, water and wine in a large, heavy-bottom pan and cook, covered, over high heat, shaking the pan occasionally, for 3–4 minutes, or until the clams have opened. Discard any clams that remain closed.

Remove the clams with a slotted spoon and set aside to cool slightly. Strain the cooking liquid through a cheesecloth-lined strainer into a small pan. Bring to a boil and cook until reduced by about half, then remove from heat. Meanwhile, remove the clams from their shells and set aside.

Bring a large pan of lightly salted water to a boil. Add the pasta, return to a boil, and cook for 8–10 minutes until tender but still firm to the bite.

Meanwhile, heat the oil in a large, heavy-bottom skillet, add the garlic, and cook, stirring frequently, for 2 minutes. Add the parsley and the reduced cooking liquid and let simmer gently.

Drain the pasta and add to the skillet with the clams. Season to taste with salt and pepper and cook, stirring constantly, for 4 minutes until the pasta is coated and the clams have heated through. Transfer to a warmed serving dish and serve at once.

serves 4 | *prep* 30 minutes | *cook* 35 minutes

SEAFOOD RISOTTO

8 oz/225 g raw shrimp, in their shells
8 oz/225 g live clams
8 oz/225 g live mussels
2 garlic cloves, halved
1 lemon, sliced
2¹/2 cups water
¹/2 cup unsalted butter

1 tbsp olive oil
1 onion, finely chopped
2 tbsp chopped fresh flat-leaf parsley
scant 1²/3 cups risotto rice
¹/2 cup dry white wine
8 oz/225 g prepared squid, cut into
    small pieces or rings

4 tbsp Marsala
salt and pepper

Pull the heads off the shrimp, then peel off the shells. Wrap the heads and shells in a square of cheesecloth and gently pound with a pestle or the side of a rolling pin, reserving any liquid they may yield. Using a sharp knife, make a slit along the underside of each shrimp, then pull out the dark vein and discard. Set the shrimp aside until required. Scrub the clams under cold running water. Clean the mussels by scrubbing or scraping the shells and pulling out any beards that are attached to them. Discard any mussels or clams with broken shells or any that refuse to close when tapped. Put into a colander and rinse under cold running water.

Put the garlic, lemon, mussels, and clams in a large, heavy-bottom pan and add the cheesecloth-wrapped shells and any reserved liquid. Pour in the water, cover tightly, and bring to a boil over high heat. Cook, shaking the pan occasionally, for 3–4 minutes, or until the mussels and clams have opened. Discard any that remain closed. Transfer the mussels and clams to a bowl and strain the cooking liquid through a cheesecloth-lined strainer into a measuring cup. Make up to 2¹/2 cups with water.

Pour the liquid into a clean pan. Bring to a boil, then reduce the heat and let simmer gently.

Melt 2 tablespoons of the butter with the oil in a large, heavy-bottom pan over low heat, add the onion and half the parsley, and cook, stirring occasionally, for 5 minutes until softened. Add the rice and cook, stirring constantly, for 2–3 minutes until all the grains are coated and glistening.

Add the wine and cook, stirring constantly, until it has almost completely evaporated. Add a ladleful of the hot shellfish cooking liquid and cook, still stirring constantly, until it has been absorbed. Continue cooking, stirring and adding the liquid, a ladleful at a time, for 20 minutes, or until the rice is tender and all the liquid has been absorbed.

About 5 minutes before the rice is ready, melt 4 tablespoons of the remaining butter in a heavy-bottom pan over medium heat. Add the squid and cook, stirring frequently, for 3 minutes, then add the reserved shrimp and cook for an additional 2–3 minutes until the squid is opaque and the shrimp turn pink. Stir in the Marsala, bring to a boil, and cook until all the liquid has evaporated.

Stir the seafood into the rice, add the remaining butter and parsley, and season to taste with salt and pepper. Heat through briefly and serve at once.

serves 6 | prep 25 minutes, plus 40 minutes' chilling and resting | cook 50–55 minutes

CRAB & WATERCRESS TART

Lightly grease a 9-inch/23-cm loose-bottom fluted tart pan. Sift the flour with the salt into a food processor, add the butter, and process until the mixture resembles fine bread crumbs. Tip the mixture into a large bowl and add a little cold water, just enough to bring the dough together. Turn out onto a lightly floured counter. Roll out to 3¼ inches/8 cm larger than the pan. Line the pan with the dough and trim the edge. Line the tart shell with parchment paper and fill with dried beans. Let chill in the refrigerator for 30 minutes. Meanwhile, preheat the oven to 375°F/190°C.

Remove the tart shell from the refrigerator and bake in the preheated oven for 10 minutes. Remove the paper and beans and bake the tart shell for an additional 5 minutes. Remove from the oven and reduce the oven temperature to 325°F/160°C.

Arrange the crabmeat and watercress in the tart shell, reserving a few watercress leaves for garnishing. Whisk the milk, eggs, and egg yolks together in a bowl. Bring the cream to simmering point in a pan and pour over the egg mixture, whisking all the time. Season to taste with salt and pepper and stir in the nutmeg and chives. Carefully pour over the crab and watercress and sprinkle over the cheese. Bake for 35–40 minutes until golden and set. Let the tart rest for 10 minutes before serving, garnished with the reserved watercress.

PIE DOUGH
scant 1 cup all-purpose flour, plus
   extra for dusting
pinch of salt
4 tbsp cold butter, diced, plus extra
   for greasing
ice-cold water

FILLING
10½ oz/300 g fresh white and brown
   crabmeat, thawed if frozen
1 bunch of watercress, leaves picked
   from the stems
¼ cup milk
2 large eggs plus 3 egg yolks
scant 1 cup heavy cream
½ tsp ground nutmeg
½ bunch of fresh chives, snipped
2 tbsp freshly grated Parmesan
   cheese
salt and pepper

serves 4–6 | prep 20 minutes | cook 40 minutes

CRAB SOUFFLE

¼ cup dried bread crumbs
3 tbsp butter, plus extra
   for greasing
1 small onion, finely chopped
1 garlic clove, crushed
2 tsp mustard powder
scant ½ cup all-purpose flour
1 cup milk
1¾ oz/50 g Gruyère cheese, grated
3 eggs, separated
8 oz/ 225 g fresh crabmeat, thawed
   if frozen
2 tbsp snipped fresh chives
pinch of cayenne pepper
salt and pepper

Preheat the oven to 400°F/200°C. Generously grease a 6-cup soufflé dish. Add the bread crumbs and shake around the dish to coat completely, shaking out any excess. Set aside on a baking sheet.

Melt the butter in a large pan over low heat, add the onion, and cook, stirring occasionally, for 8 minutes, until softened but not browned. Add the garlic and cook, stirring, for 1 minute. Then add the mustard powder and flour and continue stirring for another minute. Gradually add the milk, stirring constantly, until smooth. Increase the heat slightly and bring slowly to a boil, stirring constantly. Let simmer gently for 2 minutes. Remove from the heat and stir in the cheese. Let cool slightly.

Lightly beat in the egg yolks, then fold in the crabmeat, chives, cayenne, and salt and pepper to taste.

Whisk the egg whites in a clean, greasefree bowl until they hold stiff peaks. Add a large spoonful of the egg whites to the crab mixture and fold together to slacken. Add the remaining egg whites and fold together carefully but thoroughly. Spoon into the prepared dish.

Cook in the preheated oven for 25 minutes until well risen and golden. Serve at once.

6

Healthful, colorful, flavorful—you simply cannot go wrong with this range of easy yet imaginative fish-based salads. Some are light, refreshing summertime dishes, as you would expect, but others featuring rice, couscous, pasta, noodles, and potatoes offer more substantial fare to serve as a main meal at any time of year.

SALADS

Salade Niçoise is a familiar favorite, but there are other variations on the same theme using fresh tuna steaks cooked in moments in a stovetop grill pan. Besides beans, canned and fresh, creamy avocado and tender asparagus spears provide perfect support for the star ingredient. But for a taste of the exotic, try Chinese Shrimp Salad, with mango, and Cantaloupe & Crab Salad.

serves 4 | prep 25 minutes, plus 6 hours' chilling | cook 10 minutes

MACKEREL & POTATO SALAD

4¹/₂ oz/125 g new potatoes, scrubbed
and diced
8 oz/225 g mackerel fillets, skinned
5 cups water
1 bay leaf
1 slice of lemon
1 eating apple, cored and diced
1 shallot, thinly sliced
3 tbsp white wine vinegar
1 tsp sunflower-seed oil
1¹/₂ tsp superfine sugar
¹/₄ tsp Dijon mustard
salt and pepper

TO SERVE
2 tbsp lowfat plain yogurt
¹/₄ cucumber, thinly sliced
1 bunch of watercress
1 tbsp snipped fresh chives

Steam the potatoes over a pan of simmering water for 10 minutes, or until tender. Meanwhile, using a sharp knife, remove the skin from the mackerel fillets and discard. Cut the fish into bite-size pieces. Bring the water to a boil in a large, shallow pan, then reduce the heat so that it is just simmering and add the fish pieces, bay leaf, and lemon. Poach for 3 minutes, or until the flesh of the fish is opaque. Remove with a slotted spoon and transfer to a serving dish.

Drain the potatoes and transfer to a large bowl. Add the apple and shallot and mix well, then spoon the mixture over the fish.

Mix the vinegar, oil, sugar, and mustard together in a pitcher, season to taste with salt and pepper, and whisk thoroughly. Pour the dressing over the potato mixture. Cover and let chill in the refrigerator for up to 6 hours.

To serve, spread the yogurt over the salad, then arrange the cucumber decoratively on top. Add sprigs of watercress and sprinkle with the chives.

serves 4 | prep 10 minutes | cook 10 minutes

SMOKED HADDOCK SALAD

12 oz/350 g smoked haddock fillet,
  skinned
4 tbsp olive oil
1 tbsp lemon juice
2 tbsp sour cream
1 tbsp hot water
2 tbsp snipped fresh chives, plus extra
  to garnish
1 plum tomato, peeled, seeded,
  and diced
8 quail's eggs
4 thick slices whole grain or multigrain
  bread
4 oz/115 g mixed salad greens
salt and pepper

Fill a large skillet with water and bring
to a boil. Add the smoked haddock fillet,
cover, and remove the skillet from the heat.
Let stand for 10 minutes until the fish is
tender. Remove with a slotted spoon and
drain on a plate. Flake the fish, removing
and discarding any small bones. Set aside.
Discard the cooking liquid.

Meanwhile, whisk the oil, lemon juice, sour
cream, hot water, chives, and salt and pepper
to taste together in a pitcher. Stir in the
tomato. Set aside.

Bring a small pan of water to a boil. Carefully
lower the quail's eggs into the water and cook
for 3–4 minutes from when the water returns
to a boil (3 minutes for a slightly soft center,
4 minutes for a firm center). Drain at once
and refresh under cold running water.
Carefully shell the eggs, cut in half lengthwise
and set aside.

Toast the bread and put a slice on each of
4 serving plates. Top with the salad greens,
then the flaked fish and finally the quail's
eggs. Spoon over the dressing and garnish
with a few extra chives.

serves 4 | prep 20 minutes, plus 20 minutes' cooling | cook 10–12 minutes

SALADE NICOISE

Bring 2 pans of water to a boil. Add the eggs to 1 pan and return to a boil. Reduce the heat and cook for 10 minutes. Meanwhile, put the beans in the other pan. Bring to a boil and blanch for 3 minutes, then drain and plunge into cold water. Drain again and let cool. When the eggs are cooked, drain and plunge into cold water. Drain again and let cool.

To make the dressing, combine the olive oil, vinegar, honey, and garlic in a small bowl. Season to taste with salt and pepper and stir well together.

Divide the bell pepper, tomatoes, onion, parsley, and cilantro between 4 serving dishes. Halve the olives and the beans, shell and quarter the eggs, and add them all to the salad. Drain the tuna and anchovies and add to the salad. Drizzle over the dressing and garnish with capers and parsley sprigs. Cover with plastic wrap and let chill in the refrigerator until required.

4 eggs
7 oz/200 g green beans
1 green bell pepper, seeded and sliced
4 tomatoes, cut into wedges
1 red onion, halved and sliced
1 tbsp chopped fresh parsley
1 tbsp chopped fresh cilantro
1/4 cup black olives, pitted
14 oz/400 g canned tuna in brine
1 3/4 oz/50 g anchovy fillets in oil

DRESSING
5 tbsp extra virgin olive oil
3 tbsp red wine vinegar
1/2 tsp honey
1 garlic clove, chopped
salt and pepper

TO GARNISH
capers, rinsed
fresh parsley sprigs

serves 4 | prep 15 minutes | cook 30 minutes

MOROCCAN COUSCOUS SALAD

scant 1¼ cups couscous
1 cinnamon stick, about 2 inches/
   5 cm long
2 tsp coriander seeds
1 tsp cumin seeds
2 tbsp olive oil
1 small onion, finely chopped
2 garlic cloves, finely chopped
½ tsp ground turmeric
pinch of cayenne pepper
1 tbsp lemon juice
scant ⅓ cup golden raisins
3 ripe plum tomatoes, chopped
3 oz/85 g cucumber, chopped
4 scallions, sliced
7 oz/200 g canned tuna in olive oil,
   drained and flaked
3 tbsp chopped fresh cilantro
salt and pepper

Prepare the couscous according to the package instructions, omitting any butter. Transfer to a large bowl and set aside.

Heat a small, dry skillet over high heat and add the cinnamon stick, coriander seeds, and cumin seeds. Cook, shaking the skillet frequently, until the seeds begin to pop and smell fragrant. Remove from the heat and pour the seeds into a mortar. Grind with a pestle to a fine powder. Alternatively, grind in a spice grinder. Set aside.

Heat the oil in a clean skillet over low heat, add the onion, and cook, stirring frequently, for 7–8 minutes until softened and lightly browned. Add the garlic and cook, stirring, for an additional minute. Stir in the roasted and ground spices, turmeric, and cayenne pepper and cook, stirring, for another minute. Remove from the heat and stir in the lemon juice. Add this mixture to the couscous and mix together well, making sure that all of the grains are coated.

Add the golden raisins, tomatoes, cucumber, scallions, tuna, and cilantro. Season to taste with salt and pepper and mix together. Let cool completely. Serve at room temperature.

serves 4 | prep 10 minutes | cook 5–10 minutes

WARM TUNA & KIDNEY BEAN SALAD

4 fresh tuna steaks, about 6 oz/
175 g each
1 tbsp olive oil
7 oz/200 g canned kidney beans
3¹/₂ oz/100 g canned corn kernels
2 scallions, thinly sliced
salt and pepper

DRESSING
5 tbsp extra virgin olive oil
3 tbsp balsamic vinegar
1 tbsp lime juice
1 garlic clove, chopped
1 tbsp chopped fresh cilantro
salt and pepper

TO GARNISH
fresh cilantro sprigs
lime wedges

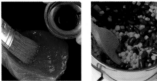

Heat a stovetop ridged grill pan over high
heat. Lightly brush the tuna steaks with olive
oil, then season to taste with salt and pepper.
Cook the steaks for 2 minutes, then turn over
and cook on the other side for an additional
2 minutes for rare or up to 4 minutes for
well done. Remove from the heat and let
cool slightly.

Meanwhile, heat the beans and corn
according to the can instructions, then drain.

To make the dressing, put all the dressing
ingredients in a small bowl. Stir together well.

Put the beans, corn, and scallions in a large
bowl, pour over half the dressing, and mix
together well. Divide the bean and corn salad
between 4 individual serving plates, then top
each one with a tuna steak. Drizzle over the
remaining dressing, garnish with cilantro
sprigs and lime wedges, and serve at once.

serves 4–6 | prep 15 minutes | cook 12 minutes

TUNA & TWO-BEAN SALAD

7 oz/200 g green beans
14 oz/400 g canned small white
  beans, such as cannellini, rinsed
  and drained
4 scallions, finely chopped
2 fresh tuna steaks, about 8 oz/225 g
  each and ³/₄ inch/2 cm thick
olive oil, for brushing
9 oz/250 g cherry tomatoes, halved
lettuce leaves
fresh mint and parsley sprigs,
  to garnish
country-style crusty bread, to serve

DRESSING
handful of fresh mint leaves, shredded
handful of fresh parsley leaves,
  chopped
1 garlic clove, crushed
4 tbsp extra virgin olive oil
1 tbsp red wine vinegar
salt and pepper

First, make the dressing. Put the mint leaves, parsley leaves, garlic, olive oil, and vinegar into a screw-top jar, add salt and pepper to taste, and shake until blended. Pour into a large bowl and set aside.

Bring a pan of lightly salted water to a boil. Add the green beans and cook for 3 minutes. Add the white beans and cook for another 4 minutes until the green beans are tender-crisp and the white beans are heated through. Drain well and add to the bowl with the dressing and scallions. Toss together.

To cook the tuna, heat a stovetop ridged grill pan over high heat. Lightly brush the tuna steaks with oil, then season to taste with salt and pepper. Cook the steaks for 2 minutes, then turn over and cook on the other side for an additional 2 minutes for rare or up to 4 minutes for well done.

Remove the tuna from the grill pan and let rest for 2 minutes, or until completely cool. When ready to serve, add the tomatoes to the bean mixture and toss lightly. Line a serving platter with lettuce leaves and pile on the bean salad. Flake the tuna over the top. Serve warm or at room temperature with plenty of bread, garnished with the herbs.

serves 4 | prep 15 minutes | cook 15 minutes

TUNA & HERBED FUSILLI SALAD

7 oz/200 g dried fusilli
1 red bell pepper, seeded
    and quartered
5½ oz/150 g asparagus spears
1 red onion, sliced
4 tomatoes, sliced
7 oz/200 g canned tuna in brine,
    drained and flaked

DRESSING

6 tbsp basil-flavored oil or
    extra virgin olive oil
3 tbsp white wine vinegar
1 tbsp lime juice
1 tsp mustard
1 tsp honey
4 tbsp chopped fresh basil, plus extra
    sprigs to garnish

Bring a large pan of lightly salted water to a boil. Add the pasta, return to a boil, and cook for 8–10 minutes until tender but still firm to the bite.

Meanwhile, put the bell pepper quarters under a preheated hot broiler and cook for 10–12 minutes until the skins begin to blacken. Transfer to a plastic bag, seal, and set aside.

Bring a separate pan of water to a boil, add the asparagus, and blanch for 4 minutes. Drain and plunge into cold water, then drain again. Remove the pasta from the heat, drain, and set aside to cool. Remove the bell pepper quarters from the bag and peel off the skins. Slice the bell pepper into strips.

To make the dressing, put all the dressing ingredients in a large bowl and stir together well. Add the pasta, bell pepper strips, asparagus, onion, tomatoes, and tuna. Toss together gently, then divide between serving bowls. Garnish with basil sprigs and serve.

serves 4 | *prep 20 minutes* | *cook no cooking required*

SMOKED SALMON & WILD ARUGULA SALAD

1¾ oz/50 g wild arugula leaves
1 tbsp chopped fresh flat-leaf parsley
2 scallions, finely diced
2 large avocados
1 tbsp lemon juice
9 oz/250 g smoked salmon
lime wedges, to serve

LIME MAYONNAISE
⅔ cup mayonnaise
2 tbsp lime juice
finely grated rind of 1 lime
1 tbsp chopped fresh flat-leaf parsley,
   plus extra sprigs to garnish

Shred the arugula and arrange in 4 individual salad bowls or on 4 small plates. Sprinkle over the chopped parsley and scallions.

Halve, peel, and pit the avocados and cut into thin slices or small chunks. Brush with the lemon juice to prevent discoloration, then divide between the salad bowls. Mix together gently. Cut the smoked salmon into strips and sprinkle over the top.

Put the mayonnaise in a bowl, then add the lime juice and rind and the chopped parsley. Mix together well. Spoon some of the lime mayonnaise on top of each salad, garnish with parsley sprigs, and serve with lime wedges for squeezing over.

serves 4 | *prep* 15 minutes | *cook* 5 minutes

SMOKED SALMON, ASPARAGUS
& AVOCADO SALAD

7 oz/200 g asparagus spears
1 large avocado
1 tbsp lemon juice
large handful of arugula leaves
8 oz/225 g smoked salmon
1 red onion, finely sliced
1 tbsp chopped fresh flat-leaf parsley,
  plus extra sprigs to garnish
1 tbsp snipped fresh chives
lemon wedges, to garnish
whole wheat bread, to serve

DRESSING
1 garlic clove, chopped
4 tbsp extra virgin olive oil
2 tbsp white wine vinegar
1 tbsp lemon juice
pinch of sugar
1 tsp mustard

Bring a large pan of salted water to a boil, add the asparagus, and blanch for 4 minutes. Drain and plunge into cold water, then drain again. Set aside to cool.

To make the dressing, combine all the dressing ingredients in a small bowl and stir together well. Halve, peel, and pit the avocado and cut into bite-size pieces. Brush with the lemon juice to prevent discoloration.

To assemble the salad, arrange the arugula leaves on individual serving plates and top with the asparagus and avocado. Cut the smoked salmon into strips and arrange over the top of the salads, then sprinkle over the onion and herbs. Drizzle over the dressing, then garnish with parsley sprigs and lemon wedges. Serve with whole wheat bread.

serves 4 | prep 10 minutes, plus 10 minutes' cooling | cook 35 minutes

SHRIMP & RICE SALAD

generous ³/₄ cup mixed long-grain and
    wild rice
12 oz/350 g cooked shelled shrimp
1 mango, peeled, pitted, and diced
4 scallions, sliced
¹/₄ cup slivered almonds
1 tbsp finely chopped fresh mint
salt and pepper

DRESSING
1 tbsp extra virgin olive oil
2 tsp lime juice
1 garlic clove, crushed
1 tsp honey
salt and pepper

Bring a large pan of lightly salted water to a
boil. Add the rice, return to a boil, and cook
for 35 minutes, or until tender. Drain, then
transfer to a large bowl and stir in the shrimp.

To make the dressing, combine the olive oil,
lime juice, garlic, and honey in a large pitcher,
season to taste with salt and pepper, and
whisk until well blended. Pour the dressing
over the rice and shrimp mixture and let cool.

Add the mango, scallions, almonds, and mint
to the salad and season to taste with pepper.
Stir thoroughly, transfer to a large serving
dish, and serve.

serves 4 | prep 10 minutes | cook 15 minutes

CHINESE SHRIMP SALAD

9 oz/250 g dried fine egg noodles
3 tbsp sunflower-seed oil
1 tbsp sesame oil
1 tbsp sesame seeds
generous 1 cup bean sprouts
1 mango, peeled, pitted, and sliced
6 scallions, sliced
2¾ oz/75 g radishes, sliced
12 oz/350 g cooked shelled shrimp
2 tbsp light soy sauce
1 tbsp sherry

Put the noodles in a large, heatproof bowl and pour over enough boiling water to cover. Let stand for 10 minutes.

Drain the noodles thoroughly and pat dry with paper towels.

Heat the sunflower-seed oil in a large, preheated wok. Add the noodles and stir-fry for 5 minutes, tossing frequently.

Remove the wok from the heat and add the sesame oil, sesame seeds, and bean sprouts, tossing to mix well.

Mix the mango, scallions, radishes, shrimp, soy sauce, and sherry together in a separate bowl.

Toss the shrimp mixture with the noodles. Alternatively, arrange the noodles around the edge of a serving plate and pile the shrimp mixture into the center. Serve at once.

serves 4 | prep 15 minutes | cook 5 minutes

THAI NOODLE SALAD WITH SHRIMP

Put the noodles in a large, heatproof bowl and pour over enough boiling water to cover. Let stand for about 4 minutes, or until soft. Drain and rinse under cold running water. Drain again and set aside.

Bring a pan of water to a boil. Add the snow peas, return to a boil, and blanch for 1 minute. Drain and rinse under cold running water until cold. Drain again and set aside.

Whisk the lime juice, fish sauce, sugar, ginger, chili, and cilantro together in a large bowl. Stir in the cucumber and scallions. Add the drained noodles, snow peas, and shelled shrimp. Toss the salad gently together.

Divide the noodle salad between 4 large plates. Sprinkle with chopped cilantro and the peanuts, if using, then garnish each plate with a whole shrimp and a slice of lemon. Serve at once.

3 oz/85 g dried rice vermicelli noodles or rice sticks
6 oz/175 g snow peas, cut crosswise in half if large
5 tbsp lime juice
4 tbsp Thai fish sauce
1 tbsp sugar, or to taste
1-inch/2.5-cm piece fresh gingerroot, finely chopped
1 fresh red chili, seeded and thinly sliced diagonally
4 tbsp chopped fresh cilantro or mint, plus extra to garnish
4-inch/10-cm piece cucumber, peeled, seeded, and diced
2 scallions, thinly sliced diagonally
16–20 large cooked shelled shrimp
2 tbsp chopped unsalted peanuts or cashews (optional)

TO GARNISH
4 cooked shrimp, in their shells
lemon slices

serves 4 | *prep* 15 minutes, plus 45 minutes' chilling | *cook* 6–8 minutes

SEAFOOD SALAD

9 oz/250 g live mussels
12 oz/350 g live scallops, shucked
  and cleaned
9 oz/250 g prepared squid, cut into
  rings and tentacles
1 red onion, halved and finely sliced
10¹/₂ oz/300 g asparagus spears,
  blanched and cut into small pieces

DRESSING
4 tbsp extra virgin olive oil
2 tbsp white wine vinegar
1 tbsp lemon juice
1 garlic clove, finely chopped
1 tbsp chopped fresh flat-leaf parsley,
  plus extra sprigs to garnish
salt and pepper

TO GARNISH
lemon wedges
capers, rinsed (optional)
whole cooked baby squid (optional)

Clean the mussels by scrubbing or scraping the shells and pulling out any beards that are attached to them. Discard any with broken shells or any that refuse to close when tapped. Put the mussels in a colander and rinse well under cold running water. Put them in a large pan with just the water that clings to their shells and cook, covered, over high heat, shaking the pan occasionally, for 3–4 minutes, or until the mussels have opened. Discard any mussels that remain closed. Strain the mussels, reserving the cooking liquid. Refresh the mussels under cold running water, drain, and set aside.

Return the reserved cooking liquid to the pan and bring to a boil, add the scallops and squid, and cook for 3 minutes. Remove from the heat and drain. Refresh under cold running water and drain again. Remove the mussels from their shells. Put them in a bowl with the scallops and squid and let cool. Cover with plastic wrap and let chill in the refrigerator for 45 minutes.

Divide the seafood between 4 serving plates. Top with the onion and asparagus. Combine all the dressing ingredients in a small bowl, then drizzle over the salad. Garnish with parsley sprigs and lemon wedges, and capers and whole baby squid, if desired.

serves 4 | *prep* 25 minutes, plus 45 minutes' chilling | *cook* 10 minutes

SEAFOOD & SPINACH SALAD

1 lb 2 oz/500 g live mussels, scrubbed
and debearded
3¹/₂ oz/100 g raw shrimp, shelled
and deveined
12 oz/350 g live scallops, shucked
and cleaned
1 lb 2 oz/500 g baby spinach leaves
4 tbsp water
3 scallions, sliced
lemon wedges, to garnish

DRESSING
4 tbsp extra virgin olive oil
2 tbsp white wine vinegar
1 tbsp lemon juice
1 tsp finely grated lemon rind
1 garlic clove, chopped
1 tbsp grated fresh gingerroot
1 small fresh red chili, seeded
and sliced
1 tbsp chopped fresh cilantro, plus
extra sprigs to garnish
salt and pepper

Put the mussels in a large pan with a little
water and cook, covered, over high heat,
shaking the pan occasionally, for 3–4 minutes,
or until the mussels have opened. Discard
any mussels that remain closed. Strain the
mussels, reserving the cooking liquid.

Return the reserved cooking liquid to the pan
and bring to a boil, add the shrimp and
scallops, and cook for 3 minutes. Remove
from the heat and drain. Remove the mussels
from their shells. Refresh the mussels, shrimp,
and scallops under cold running water, drain,
and put them in a large bowl. Let cool, then
cover with plastic wrap and let chill in the
refrigerator for 45 minutes.

Meanwhile, rinse the spinach leaves and
transfer them to a pan with the water. Cook
over high heat for 1 minute. Transfer to a
colander, refresh under cold running water,
and drain.

To make the dressing, combine all the
dressing ingredients in a small bowl. Divide
the spinach between 4 serving dishes, then
sprinkle over half the scallions. Top with the
mussels, shrimp, and scallops, then sprinkle
over the remaining scallions. Drizzle over
the dressing, garnish with cilantro sprigs
and lemon wedges, and serve.

serves 4 | *prep 10 minutes, plus 30 minutes' chilling* | *cook no cooking required*

CRAB & CITRUS SALSA

9 oz/250 g canned or fresh crabmeat,
   drained if canned and thawed if
   frozen, flaked
1 red bell pepper, seeded
   and chopped
4 tomatoes, chopped
3 scallions, chopped
1 tbsp chopped fresh flat-leaf parsley,
   plus extra sprigs to garnish
1 fresh red chili, seeded and chopped
3 tbsp lime juice
3 tbsp orange juice
salt and pepper
lime wedges, to garnish

TO SERVE
thin carrot sticks
thin celery sticks
tortilla chips

Put the crabmeat, bell pepper, tomatoes,
scallions, parsley, and chili in a large,
nonmetallic bowl. Add the lime juice and
orange juice, season to taste with salt and
pepper, and mix well. Cover with plastic wrap
and let chill in the refrigerator for 30 minutes
to allow the flavors to combine.

Remove the salsa from the refrigerator.
Garnish with parsley sprigs and lime wedges
and serve with thin carrot and celery sticks
and tortilla chips for dipping.

serves 4 | prep 15 minutes | cook no cooking required

CANTALOUPE & CRAB SALAD

12 oz/350 g fresh crabmeat, thawed
  if frozen
5 tbsp low-fat mayonnaise
¼ cup low-fat plain yogurt
4 tsp extra virgin olive oil
4 tsp lime juice
1 scallion, finely chopped
4 tsp finely chopped fresh flat-leaf
  parsley, plus extra sprigs to garnish
pinch of cayenne pepper
1 cantaloupe melon
2 radicchio heads, separated
  into leaves

Put the crabmeat in a large bowl and pick over it very carefully to remove any remaining shell or cartilage, but try not to break the meat up.

Put the mayonnaise, yogurt, oil, lime juice, scallion, chopped parsley, and cayenne pepper in a separate bowl and mix together until well blended. Fold in the crabmeat.

Halve the melon and remove and discard the seeds. Thinly slice, then cut off the rind with a sharp knife.

Arrange the melon slices and radicchio leaves on 4 large serving plates, then arrange the crabmeat mixture on top. Garnish with a few parsley sprigs and serve.

7

Fish takes center stage in this next selection of recipes, providing simple yet sophisticated dishes for entertaining in high style and everyday meals for family and friends. Along with such fish staples as salmon, trout, cod, and flounder, skate, hake, sole, angler fish, red snapper, and porgy all make a unique culinary contribution.

HEARTY MAIN DISHES

Fish pie never loses its appeal, and here you can enjoy it in its many guises—cloaked in rich puff pastry in Salmon Coulibiac and Flaky Pastry Fish Pie, or topped with crisp-baked, creamy mash in Fisherman's Pie. But you may be looking for something more challenging on the taste buds, in which case Thai-style Fish Curry with Rice Noodles, aromatic Moroccan Fish Tagine, and piquant Whole Deep-Fried Fish with Soy & Ginger are sure to satisfy.

serves 4 | prep 15 minutes | cook 35–50 minutes

BAKED MACKEREL STUFFED
WITH RAISINS & PINE NUTS

3 tbsp olive oil, plus extra for oiling
1 onion, finely chopped
1³/₄ oz fresh bread crumbs
generous ¹/₃ cup raisins, chopped
²/₃ cup pine nuts
grated rind and juice of 1 lemon
1 tbsp chopped fresh dill
2 tbsp chopped fresh flat-leaf parsley
1 egg, beaten
4 mackerel, cleaned, about 12 oz/
    350 g each
salt and pepper
lemon wedges, to garnish

Preheat the oven to 375°F/190°C. Oil a shallow ovenproof dish large enough to hold the fish in a single layer.

To make the stuffing, heat 2 tablespoons of the oil in a large, heavy-bottom skillet, add the onion, and cook, stirring frequently, for 5 minutes until softened. Remove from the heat.

Put the bread crumbs, raisins, pine nuts, lemon rind, dill, parsley, and salt and pepper to taste in a large bowl. Add the onion and egg and mix well together.

Press the stuffing mixture into the cavity of the fish and transfer to the prepared dish. Using a sharp knife, make diagonal slashes along each fish. Drizzle over the lemon juice and the remaining oil.

Bake the fish, uncovered, in the preheated oven, basting twice during cooking, for 30–45 minutes until tender. Serve hot, garnished with lemon wedges.

serves 4 | prep 30 minutes | cook 45–50 minutes

SALMON COULIBIAC

¼ cup long-grain white rice
3 eggs
2 tbsp vegetable oil
1 onion, finely chopped
1 garlic clove, crushed
1 tsp finely grated lemon rind
2 tbsp chopped fresh parsley
1 tbsp chopped fresh dill
1 lb/450 g salmon fillet, skinned
   and cubed
1 lb 2 oz/500 g ready-made
   puff pastry

all-purpose flour, for dusting
beaten egg, for sealing
   and glazing

QUICK HOLLANDAISE SAUCE
¾ cup butter, plus extra
   for greasing
1 tbsp wine vinegar
2 tbsp lemon juice
3 egg yolks
salt and pepper

Preheat the oven to 400°F/200°C. Lightly grease a baking sheet. Bring a pan of lightly salted water to a boil. Add the rice, return to a boil, and cook for 7–8 minutes until tender. Drain well and set aside. Meanwhile, bring a small pan of water to a boil. Add the eggs, return to a boil, and cook for 8 minutes. Drain and refresh under cold water. When cool enough to handle, shell and slice thinly.

Heat the oil in a skillet over medium heat, add the onion, and cook, stirring frequently, for 5 minutes until softened. Add the garlic and cook, stirring, for an additional 30 seconds. Add to the rice with the lemon rind, parsley, dill, and salmon.

Roll out the pastry on a lightly floured counter to a rectangle measuring 16 x 12 inches/40 x 30 cm. Transfer to the prepared baking sheet. Spoon half the filling onto one half of the pastry, leaving a border about ¾ inch/2 cm. Top with the sliced eggs, then the remaining filling.

Dampen the outside edges of the pastry with a little beaten egg, then fold over the remaining pastry. Crimp the edges to seal well. Mark the pastry using a small sharp knife, taking care not to cut through the pastry. Decorate with pastry trimmings and brush with beaten egg.

Bake in the preheated oven for 30–35 minutes until risen and golden.

To make the sauce, melt the butter in a small pan over low heat. Put the vinegar and lemon juice in a separate pan and bring to a boil. Meanwhile, put the egg yolks and a pinch of salt in a blender or food processor and combine. With the motor running, gradually add the hot vinegar and lemon juice through the feed tube. When the butter starts to bubble, pour it in a steady stream into the machine until it has all been added and the sauce has thickened. Season to taste with salt and pepper. Transfer to a heatproof bowl set over a pan of hot water to keep warm.

Serve the pie hot with the sauce.

serves 4 | prep 15 minutes | cook 5–6 minutes

SALMON STEAKS WITH GREEN SAUCE

4 salmon fillets, about 5 oz/140 g
  each, skinned
2 tbsp olive oil
salt and pepper

GREEN SAUCE
2½ oz/70 g fresh flat-leaf
  parsley sprigs
8 large fresh basil leaves
2 fresh oregano sprigs or ½ tsp dried
3–4 canned anchovy fillets in oil,
  drained and chopped
2 tsp capers, rinsed
1 shallot, chopped
1 large garlic clove
2–3 tsp lemon juice, to taste
½ cup extra virgin olive oil

To make the sauce, put the parsley, basil, oregano, anchovies, capers, shallot, garlic, and lemon juice in a food processor and process until chopped. With the motor running, slowly add the extra virgin olive oil through the feed tube. Taste and adjust the seasoning, if necessary, remembering that the anchovies and capers are salty in themselves. Pour into a serving bowl, cover with plastic wrap and let chill until required.

When ready to serve, brush the salmon fillets on both sides with the olive oil and season to taste with salt and pepper. Heat a large skillet over high heat until you can feel the heat rising from the surface. Cook the salmon steaks for 3 minutes, then turn over and cook on the other side for 2–3 minutes until they feel springy and the flesh flakes easily.

Serve the hot salmon steaks with a little of the chilled sauce spooned over.

serves 6 | prep 15 minutes, plus 15 minutes–2 hours' cooling | cook 50 minutes–1 hour

POACHED SALMON

melted butter, for brushing
1 whole fresh salmon, about 4 lb/
　1.8 kg, cleaned and scaled
1 lemon, sliced
few fresh parsley sprigs, plus extra
　to garnish
1/2 cup white wine or water
salt and pepper
lemon wedges, to garnish

HOLLANDAISE SAUCE
2 tbsp white wine vinegar
2 tbsp water
6 black peppercorns
3 egg yolks
1 1/8 cups unsalted butter
2 tsp lemon juice
salt and pepper

Preheat the oven to 300°F/150°C. Line a large roasting pan with a double layer of foil and brush with butter.

Trim off the fins, then season the salmon to taste with salt and pepper, inside and out. Lay on the foil and put the lemon slices and parsley in the body cavity. Pour over the wine and gather up the foil to make a fairly loose package.

Bake in the preheated oven for 50 minutes–1 hour. Test the salmon with the tip of a knife—the flesh should flake when the fish is cooked. Remove from the oven and let stand for 15 minutes before removing from the foil to serve hot. To serve cold, leave for 1–2 hours until lukewarm, then carefully remove from the foil and peel away the skin from the top side, leaving the head and tail intact.

Meanwhile, to make the sauce, put the vinegar, water, and peppercorns in a small pan and bring to a boil, then reduce the heat and let simmer until it is reduced to 1 tablespoon (take care—this happens very quickly). Strain the vinegar and discard the peppercorns.

Put the egg yolks in a blender or food processor and process to blend. With the motor running, add the vinegar through the feed tube. Melt the butter in a small pan over high heat and heat until it almost turns brown. Again, while the motor is running, add three-quarters of the butter, the lemon juice, then the remaining butter through the feed tube. Season well with salt and pepper.

Transfer the sauce to a serving bowl or keep warm for up to 1 hour in a heatproof bowl set over a pan of hot water. To serve cold, let cool, cover, and store in the refrigerator for up to 2 days. Serve the sauce on the side with the salmon, garnished with parsley sprigs and lemon wedges.

serves 4 | prep 10 minutes, plus 15 minutes' soaking | cook 15–20 minutes

COD WITH CATALAN SPINACH

4 cod fillets, about 6 oz/175 g each
olive oil
salt and pepper
lemon wedges, to serve

CATALAN SPINACH
generous 1/3 cup raisins
3/8 cup pine nuts
4 tbsp extra virgin olive oil
3 garlic cloves, crushed
1 lb 2 oz/500 g baby spinach leaves,
  rinsed and shaken dry

To make the Catalan Spinach, put the raisins in a small bowl, cover with hot water, and set aside to soak for 15 minutes. Drain well.

Meanwhile, put the pine nuts in a skillet over medium-high heat and dry-fry, shaking the pan frequently, for 1–2 minutes until toasted and golden brown—watch closely because they burn quickly.

Heat the extra virgin olive oil in a large skillet with a tight-fitting lid over medium–high heat, add the garlic, and cook, stirring, for 2 minutes, or until golden but not browned. Remove with a slotted spoon and discard.

Add the spinach to the oil with only the water that clings to the leaves. Cover and cook for 4–5 minutes until wilted. Uncover, stir in the raisins and pine nuts, and continue cooking until all the liquid evaporates. Season to taste with salt and pepper and keep warm.

Brush the cod fillets lightly with olive oil and sprinkle with salt and pepper to taste. Put under a preheated hot broiler about 4 inches/10 cm from the heat and broil for 8–10 minutes until the flesh is opaque and flakes easily.

Divide the spinach between 4 serving plates and arrange the cod fillets on top. Serve with lemon wedges for squeezing over.

serves 4–6 | prep 25 minutes | cook 35–45 minutes

FLAKY PASTRY FISH PIE

1 lb 7 oz/650 g white fish fillets, such
  as cod or haddock, skinned
1¼ cups milk
1 bay leaf
4 peppercorns
1 small onion, finely sliced
3 tbsp butter, plus extra
  for greasing
⅓ cup all-purpose flour, plus extra
  for dusting
1 tbsp chopped fresh parsley
  or tarragon
⅔ cup light cream
2 hard-cooked eggs, coarsely chopped
14 oz/400 g ready-made puff pastry
1 egg, beaten
salt and pepper

Preheat the oven to 400°F/200°C. Grease a 5-cup pie dish.

Put the fish in a skillet and cover with the milk. Add the bay leaf, peppercorns, and onion slices. Bring to a boil, then reduce the heat and let simmer gently for 10–12 minutes.

Remove from the heat and strain off the milk into a measuring cup. Add a little extra milk, if necessary, to make up to 1¼ cups. Flake the fish into large pieces, removing and discarding any bones.

Melt the butter in a pan over low heat, add the flour and cook, stirring constantly, for 2–3 minutes. Remove from the heat and gradually stir in the reserved milk, beating well after each addition. Return the pan to the heat and cook, stirring constantly, until thickened. Cook for an additional

2–3 minutes until smooth and glossy. Add the herbs, cream, and salt and pepper to taste.

Put the fish in the pie dish, then add the hard-cooked eggs and season to taste with salt and pepper. Pour the sauce over and mix carefully.

Roll out the pastry on a lightly floured counter until just larger than the pie dish. Cut off a strip ½ inch/1 cm wide from around the edge. Moisten the rim of the dish with water and press the pastry strip onto it. Moisten the pastry collar and put on the pastry lid. Crimp the edges to seal well. If desired, garnish with the pastry trimmings shaped into leaves. Brush with the beaten egg.

Put the pie on a baking sheet and bake near the top of the preheated oven for 20–25 minutes. Cover with foil if it begins to get too brown.

serves 4 | *prep 15 minutes* | *cook 25 minutes*

ANGLER FISH PACKAGES

4 tsp olive oil
2 zucchini, sliced
1 large red bell pepper, peeled,
    seeded, and cut into strips
2 angler fish fillets, about 4¹/₂ oz/125 g
    each, skin and membrane removed
6 smoked lean bacon slices
salt and pepper

TO SERVE
freshly cooked pasta
slices of olive bread

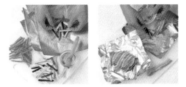

Preheat the oven to 375°F/190°C. Cut 4 large pieces of foil, about 9 inches/23 cm square. Brush lightly with a little of the oil, then divide the zucchini and bell pepper between them.

Rinse the fish fillets under cold running water and pat dry with paper towels. Cut them in half, then put 1 piece on top of each pile of zucchini and bell pepper. Cut the bacon slices in half and lay 3 pieces across each piece of fish. Season to taste with salt and pepper, drizzle over the remaining oil, and close up the packages. Seal tightly, transfer to an ovenproof dish, and bake in the preheated oven for 25 minutes.

Remove from the oven, open each foil package slightly, and serve with pasta and slices of olive bread.

serves 4 | prep 15 minutes | cook 10 minutes

FISH CURRY WITH RICE NOODLES

2 tbsp vegetable or peanut oil
1 large onion, chopped
2 garlic cloves, chopped
3 oz/85 g white mushrooms
8 oz/225 g angler fish, cut into
    1-inch/2.5-cm cubes
8 oz/225 g salmon fillets, cut into
    1-inch/2.5-cm cubes
8 oz/225 g cod fillets, cut into
    1-inch/2.5-cm cubes
2 tbsp Thai red curry paste
1³/₄ cups canned coconut milk
handful of fresh cilantro, chopped
1 tsp jaggery or brown sugar
1 tsp Thai fish sauce
4 oz/115 g dried rice noodles
3 scallions, chopped
³/₈ cup bean sprouts
few fresh Thai basil leaves

Heat the oil in a preheated wok or large skillet over medium heat, add the onion, garlic, and mushrooms and cook, stirring frequently, for 5 minutes until softened but not browned.

Add the fish, curry paste, and coconut milk and bring gently to a boil. Let simmer for 2–3 minutes before adding half the cilantro, and the sugar and fish sauce. Keep warm.

Meanwhile, soak the noodles in enough boiling water to cover in a heatproof bowl for 3–4 minutes until tender, or cook according to the package instructions. Drain well through a metal colander. Put the colander and noodles over a pan of simmering water. Add the scallions, bean sprouts, and most of the basil and steam on top of the noodles for 1–2 minutes until just wilted.

Pile the noodles onto warmed serving plates and top with the fish curry. Sprinkle the remaining cilantro and basil over the top and serve at once.

serves 4 | *prep* 10 minutes | *cook* 50 minutes–1 hour 5 minutes

MOROCCAN FISH TAGINE

2 tbsp olive oil
1 large onion, finely chopped
large pinch of saffron threads
1/2 tsp ground cinnamon
1 tsp ground coriander
1/2 tsp ground cumin
1/2 tsp ground turmeric
7 oz/200 g canned chopped tomatoes
1 1/4 cups fish stock
4 small red snapper, cleaned, boned,
    and heads and tails removed
1/3 cup pitted green olives
1 tbsp chopped preserved lemon
3 tbsp chopped fresh cilantro
salt and pepper
freshly prepared couscous, to serve

Heat the oil in a large pan or ovenproof casserole over low heat, add the onion, and cook, stirring occasionally, for 10 minutes until softened but not browned. Add the saffron, cinnamon, coriander, cumin, and turmeric and cook, stirring, for an additional 30 seconds.

Add the tomatoes and stock and stir well. Bring to a boil, then reduce the heat, cover, and let simmer for 15 minutes. Uncover and let simmer for an additional 20–35 minutes until thickened.

Cut each snapper in half, then add the pieces to the pan, pushing them into the sauce. Let simmer gently for an additional 5–6 minutes until the fish is just cooked.

Carefully stir in the olives, preserved lemon, and cilantro. Season to taste with salt and pepper and serve with couscous.

serves 2 | prep 15 minutes | cook 50 minutes

FLOUNDER FOR TWO

²/₃ cup olive oil
13 oz/375 g waxy potatoes, peeled
  and thinly sliced
1 fennel bulb, thinly sliced
2 large tomatoes, broiled, peeled,
  seeded, and chopped
2 shallots, sliced
1–2 whole flounders, cleaned, about
  3 lb/1.3 kg
4 tbsp dry white wine
2 tbsp finely chopped fresh parsley
salt and pepper
lemon wedges, to serve

Preheat the oven to 400°F/200°C. Spread
4 tablespoons of the oil over the bottom of
a shallow roasting pan large enough to hold
the flounder. Arrange the potatoes in a single
layer, then top with the fennel, tomatoes, and
shallots. Season to taste with salt and pepper.
Drizzle with an additional 4 tablespoons of
the oil. Roast the vegetables in the preheated
oven for 30 minutes.

Season the fish to taste with salt and pepper
and put on top of the vegetables. Sprinkle
with the wine and the remaining oil.

Return the roasting pan to the oven and roast
the fish, uncovered, for 20 minutes, or until
the flesh flakes easily.

To serve, skin the fish and remove the fillets.
Sprinkle the parsley over the vegetables.
Arrange 2–4 fillets on each plate, with the
vegetables spooned alongside, accompanied
by the lemon wedges for squeezing over.

serves 4 | prep 10 minutes | cook 15 minutes

PORGY EN PAPILLOTE

2 porgy, filleted
2/3 cup pitted black olives
12 cherry tomatoes, halved
4 oz/115 g green beans
handful of fresh basil leaves, plus
  extra to garnish
4 lemon slices
4 tsp olive oil
salt and pepper
boiled new potatoes, to serve

Preheat the oven to 400°F/200°C. Wash and
dry the fish fillets and set aside. Cut 4 large
rectangles of parchment paper, each
measuring about 18 x 12 inches/46 x 30 cm.
Fold in half to make a 9 x 12-inch/23 x 30-cm
rectangle. Cut this into a large heart shape
and open out.

Lay a porgy fillet on one half of the paper
heart. Top with a quarter of the olives,
tomatoes, beans, basil, and 1 lemon slice.
Drizzle over 1 teaspoon of the oil and season
well with salt and pepper.

Fold over the other half of the paper and
bring the edges of the paper together to
enclose. Repeat to make 4 packages.

Put the packages on a baking sheet and cook
in the preheated oven for 15 minutes, or until
the fish is tender.

Transfer each package to a serving plate,
unopened, allowing your guests to open
their package and enjoy the wonderful aroma.
Suggest that they garnish their portions with
basil and serve with new potatoes.

serves 4 | prep 15 minutes, plus 30 minutes' standing | cook 40 minutes

SOLE FLORENTINE

2¹/₂ cups milk
2 strips of lemon rind
2 fresh tarragon sprigs
1 fresh bay leaf
¹/₂ onion, sliced
3¹/₂ tbsp butter, plus extra
  for greasing
generous ¹/₃ cup all-purpose flour
2 tsp mustard powder
¹/₄ cup freshly grated Parmesan
  cheese
¹/₄ cups cream
pinch of freshly grated nutmeg
1 lb/450 g spinach leaves
4 Dover sole or sole quarter-cut fillets
  (two from each side of the fish),
  about 1 lb 10 oz/750 g in total
salt and pepper

TO SERVE
crisp green salad
crusty bread

Preheat the oven to 400°F/200°C. Put the milk, lemon rind, tarragon, bay leaf, and onion in a pan over medium heat and bring slowly to a boil. Remove from the heat and set aside for 30 minutes for the flavors to infuse.

Melt the butter in a separate pan over medium heat and stir in the flour and mustard powder until smooth. Strain the infused milk, discarding the lemon, herbs, and onion. Gradually beat the milk into the butter and flour until smooth. Bring slowly to a boil, stirring constantly, until thickened. Let simmer gently for 2 minutes. Remove from the heat and stir in the cheese, cream, nutmeg, and salt and pepper to taste. Cover the surface of the sauce with parchment paper or plastic wrap. Set aside.

Lightly grease a large baking dish. Bring a large pan of salted water to a boil, add the spinach, and blanch for 30 seconds. Drain and refresh under cold running water. Drain again and pat dry with paper towels. Put the spinach in a layer in the base of the dish.

Wash and dry the fish fillets. Season to taste with salt and pepper and roll up. Arrange on top of the spinach and pour over the cheese sauce. Bake in the preheated oven for 35 minutes until bubbling and golden. Serve at once with a green salad and crusty bread.

serves 4 | *prep* 5 minutes | *cook* 12 minutes

SOLE MEUNIERE

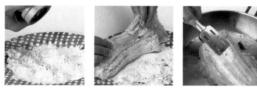

1 cup milk
generous ¾ cup all-purpose flour
1 lb 9 oz/700 g Dover sole or sole
  fillets
2 tbsp butter
1–2 tbsp sunflower-seed oil
2 tbsp chopped fresh parsley
salt and pepper
lemon wedges, to garnish

Pour the milk into a large, shallow dish.
Spread the flour out on a large, flat plate
and season to taste with salt and pepper.

Dip the sole in the milk and then in the flour,
turning to coat. Shake off any excess.

Melt the butter with the oil in a large, heavy-
bottom skillet over low heat, add the fish
fillets, and cook in batches for 2–3 minutes
on each side until lightly browned. Keep each
batch warm in a low oven while you cook the
remaining fish. Sprinkle with the parsley and
serve at once, garnished with lemon wedges.

serves 4–5 | *prep* 10 minutes, plus 10 minutes' soaking | *cook* 15–20 minutes

WHOLE DEEP-FRIED FISH
WITH SOY & GINGER

6 dried Chinese mushrooms
3 tbsp rice vinegar
2 tbsp brown sugar
3 tbsp dark soy sauce
3-inch/7.5-cm piece fresh gingerroot,
  finely chopped
4 scallions, sliced diagonally
2 tsp cornstarch
2 tbsp lime juice
1 sea bass, cleaned and scaled,
  about 2 lb 4 oz/1 kg
4 tbsp all-purpose flour
sunflower-seed oil, for deep-frying
salt and pepper
1 radish, sliced but left whole,
  to garnish

TO SERVE
shredded Napa cabbage
radish slices

Soak the dried mushrooms in hot water in a bowl for about 10 minutes, then drain well, reserving generous ¹/3 cup of the liquid. Cut into thin slices.

Mix the reserved mushroom liquid with the vinegar, sugar, and soy sauce. Put in a pan with the mushrooms and bring to a boil. Reduce the heat and let simmer for 3–4 minutes.

Add the ginger and scallions and let simmer for 1 minute. Blend the cornstarch and lime juice together, stir into the pan, and cook, stirring constantly, for 1–2 minutes until the sauce thickens and clears. Set aside.

Season the fish to taste inside and out with salt and pepper, then dust lightly with flour, carefully shaking off any excess.

Heat 1 inch/2.5 cm of oil in a wide, heavy-bottom pan to 350–375°F/180–190°C, or until a cube of bread browns in 30 seconds. Carefully lower the fish into the oil and deep-fry on one side for 3–4 minutes until golden. Use 2 metal spatulas to turn the fish carefully and deep-fry on the other side for another 3–4 minutes until golden brown.

Remove the fish, draining off the excess oil, and put on a serving plate. Reheat the sauce until boiling, then spoon it over the fish. Serve at once, surrounded by shredded Napa cabbage and sliced radishes, garnished with a sliced whole radish.

serves 4 | *prep* 5 minutes | *cook* 10–15 minutes

SKATE IN BLACK BUTTER SAUCE

4 skate wings, about 6 oz/175 g each
2 1/2 cups fish stock
1 cup dry white wine
4 tbsp butter
2 tbsp lemon juice
2 tsp capers in brine, rinsed
2 tbsp chopped fresh parsley
salt and pepper

Put the fish in a large, heavy-bottom skillet or ovenproof casserole, pour in the stock and wine, and season to taste with salt and pepper. Bring to a boil, then reduce the heat and let simmer for 10–15 minutes until the fish is tender.

Meanwhile, melt the butter in a large, heavy-bottom skillet over very low heat and cook until it turns brown but not black. Stir in the lemon juice, capers, and parsley and heat for an additional 1–2 minutes.

Transfer the skate wings to warmed serving plates with a spatula, pour the black butter sauce over, and serve at once.

serves 4 | prep 10 minutes | cook 10 minutes

HAKE IN WHITE WINE

about 2 tbsp all-purpose flour
4 hake fillets, about 5 oz/140 g each
4 tbsp extra virgin olive oil
1/2 cup dry white wine, such
  as a white Rioja
2 large garlic cloves, very finely
  chopped
6 scallions, finely sliced
1 oz/25 g fresh parsley, very finely
  chopped
salt and pepper

Preheat the oven to 450°F/230°C. Spread the flour out on a large, flat plate and season well with salt and pepper. Dredge the skin side of the hake fillets in the seasoned flour, then shake off any excess. Set aside.

Heat a shallow, ovenproof casserole over high heat until you can feel the heat rising. Add the oil and heat until a cube of bread sizzles in 30 seconds. Add the hake fillets, skin-side down, and cook for 3 minutes until the skin is golden brown.

Turn the fish over and season to taste with salt and pepper. Pour in the wine and add the garlic, scallions, and parsley. Transfer the casserole to the preheated oven and bake, uncovered, for 5 minutes, or until the flesh flakes easily. Serve the fish straight from the casserole.

serves 4 | prep 10 minutes | cook 10 minutes

BROILED RED SNAPPER WITH GARLIC

2 tbsp lemon juice
4 tbsp olive oil, plus extra for oiling
4 red snapper, cleaned and scaled
2 tbsp chopped fresh herbs, such as
    oregano, marjoram, flat-leaf parsley,
    or thyme
salt and pepper

TO GARNISH
2 garlic cloves, finely chopped
2 tbsp chopped fresh flat-leaf parsley
lemon wedges

Preheat the broiler to high. Put the lemon juice, oil, and salt and pepper to taste in a bowl and whisk together. Brush the mixture inside and on both sides of the fish and sprinkle over the herb of your choice. Transfer to an oiled broiler rack.

Cook the fish under the broiler, basting frequently and turning once, for 10 minutes, or until golden brown.

Meanwhile, mix the garlic and parsley together. Sprinkle over the top of the cooked fish and serve hot or cold, garnished with lemon wedges.

serves 6 | prep 15 minutes | cook 50 minutes–1 hour

FISHERMAN'S PIE

2 lb/900 g white fish fillets, such as
   flounder, skinned
²/₃ cup dry white wine
1 tbsp chopped fresh parsley,
   tarragon or dill
7 tbsp butter, plus extra
   for greasing
6 oz/175 g small mushrooms, sliced
6 oz/175 g cooked shelled shrimp
¹/₃ cup all-purpose flour
¹/₂ cup heavy cream
2 lb/900 g mealy potatoes, such as
   Russet Burbank, Russet Arcadia, or
   Butte, peeled and cut into chunks
salt and pepper

Preheat the oven to 350°F/180°C. Grease an 8-cup
baking dish.

Fold the fish fillets in half and put in the dish.
Season well with salt and pepper, pour over the
wine, and sprinkle over the parsley.

Cover with foil and bake in the preheated oven for
15 minutes until the fish starts to flake. Strain off the
liquid and set aside for the sauce. Increase the oven
temperature to 425°F/220°C.

Melt 1 tablespoon of the butter in a skillet over
medium heat, add the mushrooms, and cook,
stirring frequently, for 5 minutes. Spoon over the
fish. Sprinkle over the shrimp.

Heat 4 tablespoons of the remaining butter in a pan
and stir in the flour. Cook for 3–4 minutes without
browning, stirring constantly. Remove from the heat
and gradually add the reserved cooking liquid,
stirring well after each addition.

Return to the heat and slowly bring to a boil, stirring
constantly, until thickened. Add the cream and
season to taste with salt and pepper. Pour over the
fish in the dish and smooth over the surface.

Bring a large pan of salted water to a boil, add the
potatoes, and cook for 15–20 minutes. Drain
well and mash with a potato masher until smooth.
Season to taste with salt and pepper and add the
remaining butter, stirring until melted.

Pile or pipe the potato onto the fish and sauce
and bake for 10–15 minutes until golden brown.

serves 4 | *prep* 15 minutes, plus 30 minutes' marinating | *cook* 15 minutes

SICILIAN TUNA

4 tuna steaks, about 5 oz/140 g each
2 fennel bulbs, thickly sliced
  lengthwise
2 red onions, sliced
2 tbsp extra virgin olive oil
crusty rolls, to serve

MARINADE
$^1/_2$ cup extra virgin olive oil
4 garlic cloves, finely chopped
4 fresh red chilies, seeded and
  finely chopped
juice and finely grated rind of
  2 lemons
4 tbsp finely chopped fresh
  flat-leaf parsley
salt and pepper

Whisk all the marinade ingredients together in a small bowl. Put the tuna steaks in a large, shallow dish and spoon over 4 tablespoons of the marinade, turning until well coated. Cover and let marinate in the refrigerator for 30 minutes. Set aside the remaining marinade.

Heat a stovetop ridged grill pan over high heat. Put the fennel and onions in a separate bowl, add the oil, and toss well to coat. Add to the grill pan and cook for 5 minutes on each side until just beginning to color. Transfer to 4 warmed serving plates, drizzle with the reserved marinade, and keep warm.

Add the tuna steaks to the grill pan and cook, turning once, for 4–5 minutes until firm to the touch but still moist inside. Transfer the tuna to the serving plates and serve at once with crusty rolls.

serves 4 | *prep* 15 minutes | *cook* 40 minutes

SWORDFISH WITH OLIVES & CAPERS

2 tbsp all-purpose flour
4 swordfish steaks, about 8 oz/
    225 g each
generous 1/3 cup olive oil
2 garlic cloves, halved
1 onion, chopped
4 canned anchovy fillets, drained
    and chopped
4 tomatoes, peeled, seeded,
    and chopped
12 green olives, pitted and sliced
1 tbsp capers, rinsed
salt and pepper
fresh rosemary sprigs, to garnish

Spread the flour out on a large, flat plate and season to taste with salt and pepper. Coat the fish in the seasoned flour, then shake off any excess.

Heat the oil in a large, heavy-bottom skillet over low heat, add the garlic, and cook, stirring frequently, for 2–3 minutes until golden but not brown. Remove with a slotted spoon and discard.

Add the swordfish steaks to the oil and cook over medium heat for 4 minutes on each side until cooked through and golden brown. Remove with a slotted spoon and set aside.

Add the onion and anchovies to the pan and cook, mashing the anchovies with a wooden spoon, until they have turned to a purée and the onion is golden. Add the tomatoes and cook over low heat, stirring occasionally, for 20 minutes, or until the mixture has thickened.

Stir in the olives and capers and taste and adjust the seasoning, if necessary. Return the fish steaks to the pan and heat through gently. Serve garnished with rosemary sprigs.

serves 2 | prep 5 minutes | cook 15–20 minutes

TROUT WITH ALMONDS

⅓ cup all-purpose flour
2 trout, cleaned, about 12 oz/
   350 g each
4 tbsp butter
¼ cup slivered almonds
2 tbsp dry white wine
salt and pepper

Spread the flour out on a large, flat plate and season to taste with salt and pepper. Coat the trout in the seasoned flour, then shake off the excess.

Melt half the butter in a large, heavy-bottom skillet over medium heat, add the trout, and cook for 6–7 minutes on each side until tender and cooked through. Transfer to warmed plates with a spatula, cover, and keep warm.

Melt the remaining butter in the skillet, add the almonds, and cook, stirring frequently, for 2 minutes, or until golden brown. Add the wine, bring to a boil, and boil for 1 minute. Spoon the almonds and sauce over the trout and serve at once.

serves 4 | *prep* 15 minutes, plus 30 minutes' marinating | *cook* 25–30 minutes

TROUT IN LEMON & RED WINE SAUCE

Rinse the fish inside and out under cold running water and pat dry with paper towels. Put in a single layer in a nonmetallic dish. Pour the vinegar into a small pan and bring to a boil, then pour over the fish. Cover and set aside to marinate for 30 minutes.

Pour the wine and water into a pan and add the bay leaves, thyme sprigs, parsley sprigs, lemon rind, shallots, carrot, peppercorns, and cloves and salt to taste. Bring to a boil over medium–low heat.

Meanwhile, drain the trout and discard the marinade. Put the fish in a single layer in a large skillet and strain the wine mixture over them. Cover and let simmer over low heat for 15 minutes until cooked through and tender. There is no need to turn them.

4 trout, cleaned and heads removed
1 cup red wine vinegar
1¹⁄₄ cups red wine
²⁄₃ cup water
2 bay leaves
4 fresh thyme sprigs
4 fresh flat-leaf parsley sprigs,
   plus extra to garnish
thinly pared rind of 1 lemon
3 shallots, thinly sliced
1 carrot, thinly sliced
12 black peppercorns
8 cloves
6 tbsp unsalted butter, diced
1 tbsp chopped fresh flat-leaf parsley
1 tbsp chopped fresh dill
salt and pepper

Transfer the trout to individual serving plates with a spatula and keep warm. Return the cooking liquid to a boil and cook until reduced by about three-quarters. Gradually beat in the butter, a little at a time, until fully incorporated. Stir in the chopped parsley and dill and taste and adjust the seasoning, if necessary. Pour the sauce over the fish, garnish with parsley sprigs, and serve at once.

serves 6–8 | prep 25 minutes | cook 35 minutes

PAELLA

2 pinches of saffron threads
4 tbsp hot water
1¾ cups Spanish short-grain rice
16 live mussels
about 6 tbsp olive oil
6–8 unboned chicken thighs, excess
   fat removed, skin on
5 oz/140 g chorizo sausage,
   cut into ¼-inch/5-mm slices,
   casings removed
2 large onions, chopped
4 large garlic cloves, crushed
1 tsp mild or hot Spanish paprika,
   or to taste
3½ oz/100 g green beans, chopped
⅞ cup frozen peas
5 cups fish, chicken, or vegetable
   stock
16 raw shrimp, shelled and deveined
2 red bell peppers, broiled, peeled,
   and sliced
1¼ oz/35 g fresh parsley, finely
   chopped
salt and pepper

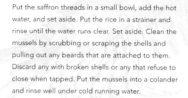

Put the saffron threads in a small bowl, add the hot water, and set aside. Put the rice in a strainer and rinse until the water runs clear. Set aside. Clean the mussels by scrubbing or scraping the shells and pulling out any beards that are attached to them. Discard any with broken shells or any that refuse to close when tapped. Put the mussels into a colander and rinse well under cold running water.

Heat half the oil in a 12-inch/30-cm paella pan or ovenproof casserole over medium–high heat, add the chicken, skin-side down, and cook for 5 minutes, or until golden and crispy. Transfer to a bowl. Add the chorizo and cook, turning frequently, for 1 minute until it starts to crisp. Add to the chicken.

Heat the remaining oil in the paella pan, add the onions, and cook, stirring frequently, for 2 minutes. Add the garlic and paprika and cook for 3 minutes until the onions are softened but not browned.

Add the drained rice, beans, and peas to the paella pan and stir until coated in oil. Return the chicken and chorizo and any accumulated juices to the pan. Stir in the stock, saffron liquid, and salt and pepper to taste and bring to a boil, stirring. Reduce the heat to low and let simmer, without stirring, for 15 minutes, or until the rice is almost tender and most of the liquid is absorbed.

Arrange the mussels, shrimp, and bell pepper strips on top, cover the pan, and continue simmering, without stirring, for 5 minutes, or until the shrimp turn pink and the mussels open.

Discard any mussels that remain closed. Taste and adjust the seasoning, if necessary. Sprinkle with chopped parsley and serve at once.

serves 4 | *prep* 15 minutes, plus 15–20 minutes' soaking | *cook* 45 minutes

STUFFED SQUID

8 sun-dried tomatoes
8 small prepared squid (bodies about
** 5 inches/13 cm long)**
1¹⁄₂ cups fresh white bread crumbs
2 tbsp capers, rinsed and
** finely chopped**
2 tbsp chopped fresh flat-leaf parsley
1 egg white
olive oil, for brushing and drizzling
3 tbsp dry white wine
salt and pepper
lemon juice, for drizzling (optional)

Preheat the oven to 325°F/160°C. Put the sun-dried tomatoes in a heatproof bowl and cover with boiling water. Set aside for 15–20 minutes.

Meanwhile, finely chop the squid tentacles and put in a separate bowl. Add the bread crumbs, capers, and parsley.

Thoroughly drain the tomatoes and pat dry with paper towels. Finely chop and add to the bread crumb mixture. Mix thoroughly and season to taste with salt and pepper. Stir in the egg white.

Spoon the bread crumb mixture into the squid body sacs, pushing it down well. Do not fill them more than about three-quarters full or they will burst during cooking. Secure the opening of each sac with a toothpick so that the stuffing will not ooze out.

Generously brush oil over an ovenproof dish large enough to hold the squid snugly in a single layer. Put the squid in the dish and pour in the wine. Cover with foil and bake in the preheated oven, turning and basting occasionally, for 45 minutes, or until tender.

Remove from the oven and set aside to cool to room temperature. To serve, remove and discard the toothpicks and slice the squid into circles. Arrange on warmed individual plates and drizzle with a little oil and either the cooled cooking juices or lemon juice.

8

Barbecued or griddled, this is the surefire way of cooking fish to enjoy all its natural flavor at its best. In the case of barbecuing, it's also an entertainment in itself, and with all the joys of eating alfresco that go with it. But the griddle offers an excellent alternative if the weather does not measure up to the occasion.

BARBECUES
AND GRIDDLES

Whole fish sizzling on the barbecue is a feast for the eye, nose, and ear in advance of the taste buds. You just need to decide on your preferred flavorings—chilies, ginger, and lime in Indonesian Spiced Fish, garlic and parsley in Stuffed Sardines, or try Bacon-Wrapped Trout. Kabobs are also enduringly appealing, and here they feature angler fish and mushrooms, shrimp and bell peppers, and scallops and corn.

serves 4 | prep 15 minutes | cook 20–30 minutes

HERRINGS WITH ORANGE TARRAGON STUFFING

1 orange
4 scallions
7/8 cup fresh whole wheat
   bread crumbs
1 tbsp chopped fresh tarragon, plus
   extra sprigs to garnish
4 herrings, cleaned and scaled
salt and pepper
green salad, to serve

TO GARNISH
2 oranges
1 tbsp sugar
1 tbsp olive oil, plus extra for oiling

Preheat the barbecue. Then start by making the stuffing. Grate the rind from half the orange using a zester. Peel and chop all the orange flesh on a plate in order to catch all the juice.

Mix the orange flesh, juice, rind, scallions, bread crumbs, and chopped tarragon together in a bowl. Season to taste with salt and pepper.

Divide the stuffing into 4 equal portions and use it to fill the body cavities of the fish.

Put each fish onto a square of lightly oiled foil and wrap the foil around the fish so that it is completely enclosed. Cook the fish over hot coals for 20–30 minutes until cooked through—the flesh should be white and firm to the touch.

Meanwhile, make the garnish. Peel and thickly slice the 2 oranges and sprinkle over the sugar. Just before the fish is cooked, drizzle the oil over the orange slices, add to the barbecue, and cook for 5 minutes.

Transfer the fish to serving plates and garnish with the barbecued orange slices and tarragon sprigs. Serve with a green salad.

serves 4 | *prep* 10 minutes, plus 2 hours' marinating | *cook* 10 minutes

SALMON TERIYAKI

4 salmon fillets, about 6 oz/175 g each

SAUCE
1 tbsp cornstarch
1/2 cup dark soy sauce
4 tbsp mirin or medium-dry sherry
2 tbsp rice or cider vinegar
2 tbsp honey

TO SERVE
1/2 cucumber
mixed salad greens, torn into pieces
4 scallions, thinly sliced diagonally

Rinse the salmon fillets under cold running water, pat dry with paper towels, and put in a large, shallow, nonmetallic dish. To make the sauce, mix the cornstarch and soy sauce together in a pitcher until a smooth paste forms, then stir in the remaining ingredients. Pour three-quarters of the sauce over the salmon, turning to coat. Cover with plastic wrap and let marinate in the refrigerator for 2 hours.

Preheat the barbecue. Cut the cucumber into thin sticks, then arrange the salad greens, cucumber, and scallions on 4 serving plates. Pour the remaining sauce into a pan and set over the barbecue to warm through.

Remove the salmon fillets with a slotted spoon and set aside the marinade. Cook the salmon over medium hot coals, brushing frequently with the reserved marinade, for 3–4 minutes on each side. Transfer the salmon fillets to the prepared serving plates and pour the warmed sauce over them. Serve at once.

serves 4 | prep 5 minutes, plus 2 hours' marinating | cook 20 minutes

BARBECUED SALMON

4 salmon steaks, about 7 oz/
   200 g each
lemon wedges, to garnish
crisp green salad leaves, to serve

MARINADE
generous 1/3 cup vegetable oil
generous 1/3 cup dry white wine
1 tbsp molasses
1 tbsp brown sugar
1 tbsp soy sauce
1 garlic clove, chopped
pinch of ground allspice
salt and pepper

Put the oil, wine, molasses, sugar, soy sauce, garlic, and allspice in a large bowl and mix until well combined. Season to taste with salt and pepper.

Rinse the salmon steaks under cold running water and pat dry with paper towels. Add the salmon to the wine mixture and turn until well coated. Cover with plastic wrap and let marinate in the refrigerator for at least 2 hours or overnight.

Preheat the barbecue. Remove the salmon steaks with a slotted spoon and set aside the marinade. Cook over hot coals, turning frequently and basting with the reserved marinade, for 10 minutes on each side, or until cooked through. About halfway through the cooking time, add the lemon wedges, and cook for 4–5 minutes, turning once. Arrange the salmon on a bed of green salad leaves, garnish with the lemon wedges, and serve.

serves 4 | *prep* 5 minutes | *cook* 10 minutes

NUT-CRUSTED HALIBUT

3 tbsp butter, melted
1 lb 10 oz/750 g halibut fillet
generous ⅓ cup pistachios, shelled
   and very finely chopped

Brush the melted butter over the halibut fillet.

Spread the nuts out on a large, flat plate.
Roll the fish in the nuts, pressing down gently.

Preheat the griddle or a stovetop grill pan
over medium heat. Cook the halibut, turning
once, for 10 minutes, or until firm but
tender—the exact cooking time will depend
on the thickness of the fillet.

Remove the fish and any loose pistachio
pieces from the heat and transfer to a large,
warmed serving platter. Serve at once.

serves 4 | prep 10 minutes | cook 6–10 minutes

COD & TOMATO PACKAGES

4 cod steaks, about 6 oz/175 g each
2 tsp extra virgin olive oil
4 tomatoes, peeled and chopped
1 oz/25 g fresh basil leaves, torn into
    small pieces
4 tbsp white wine
salt and pepper

Preheat the barbecue. Rinse the cod steaks
under cold running water and pat dry with
paper towels. Using a sharp knife, cut out and
discard the central bones. Cut 4 rectangles of
double-thickness foil, each measuring about
13 x 8 inches/33 x 20 cm. Brush with the oil.
Put a cod steak in the center of each piece
of foil.

Mix the tomatoes, basil, and wine together in
a bowl and season to taste with salt and
pepper. Divide the tomato mixture equally
between the fish and spoon on top. Bring up
the sides of the foil and fold over securely.

Cook the cod packages over hot coals for
3–5 minutes on each side. Transfer to 4 large
serving plates and serve at once in
the packages.

serves 4 | prep 10 minutes | cook 6–8 minutes

BLACKENED FISH

1 tsp black peppercorns
1 tsp fennel seeds
1 tsp cayenne pepper
1 tsp dried oregano
1 tsp dried thyme
3 garlic cloves, finely chopped
2 tbsp cornmeal
4 angler fish fillets, about
   6 oz/175 g each, skinned
3 tbsp corn oil

TO GARNISH
thinly pared strips of lime rind
lime halves

Crush the peppercorns lightly in a mortar with a pestle. Mix the crushed peppercorns, fennel seeds, cayenne, oregano, thyme, garlic, and cornmeal together in a shallow dish.

Put the angler fish, 1 fillet at a time, in the spice mixture and press gently to coat all over, then shake off any excess.

Heat the oil in a large, heavy-bottom skillet over medium heat. Add the angler fish and cook for 3–4 minutes on each side until tender and cooked through. Serve garnished with lime rind strips and lime halves.

serves 6 | prep 15 minutes | cook 20 minutes

CARIBBEAN SEA BASS

1 sea bass, cleaned and scaled, about
   3 lb 5 oz/1.5 kg
1–2 tsp olive oil
1 tsp saffron powder
½ lemon, sliced, plus extra to garnish
1 lime, sliced, plus extra to garnish
1 bunch of fresh thyme
salt and pepper

Preheat the barbecue. Rinse the sea bass inside and out under cold running water and pat dry with paper towels. Using a sharp knife, make a series of shallow diagonal slashes along each side of the fish. Brush each slash with a little of the oil, then sprinkle over the saffron powder.

Brush a large fish basket with oil and put the fish in the basket, but do not close it. Season the cavity of the fish to taste with salt and pepper. Put the lemon and lime slices and the thyme in the cavity without overfilling it.

Close the basket and cook the fish over medium hot coals for 10 minutes on each side. Carefully transfer to a large serving plate, garnish with lemon and lime slices, and serve at once.

serves 4 | *prep 15 minutes, plus 1 hour marinating* | *cook 10–15 minutes*

ANGLER FISH KABOBS

1 lb 10 oz/750 g angler fish,
   skinned and boned
8 white mushrooms
1 red onion, cut into 8 pieces
1 red or green bell pepper, seeded
   and cut into 8 pieces
2 zucchini, cut into 8 thick slices
4 tomatoes, halved, to garnish

MARINADE
1/4 cup vegetable oil,
   plus extra for basting
1 tsp paprika

Cut the angler fish into bite-size cubes.
Put in a nonmetallic dish, pour over the oil,
and sprinkle with paprika. Mix well. Cover
the dish with plastic wrap and let marinate
in the refrigerator for at least 1 hour.

Remove the angler fish from the refrigerator
and return to room temperature. Select
skewers that will fit on your griddle. Soak
wooden skewers in water for 30 minutes
before using to prevent burning. Preheat
the griddle over medium heat.

Thread the angler fish cubes onto the skewers,
alternating with the mushrooms and vegetable
pieces. Put the kabobs on the griddle and
cook, turning frequently and basting
occasionally with oil, for 10–15 minutes,
or until the fish is firm and the vegetables
tender. If you wish, place the tomato halves
on the griddle for the last 2–3 minutes.

Serve the kabobs on individual serving plates,
garnished with the tomato.

serves 4 | *prep 15 minutes* | *cook 15 minutes*

SPICY PORGY

2 porgy, filleted
2 garlic cloves, chopped
2 shallots, grated
1 small fresh red chili, seeded
  and chopped
1 tbsp lemon juice
lemon wedges, to garnish

AIOLI
4 large garlic cloves, finely chopped
2 small egg yolks
1 cup extra virgin olive oil
2 tbsp lemon juice
1 tbsp Dijon mustard
1 tbsp chopped fresh tarragon
salt and pepper

TO SERVE
crisp salad greens
raw and lightly blanched vegetables

To make the aïoli, put the garlic and egg yolks in a blender or food processor and process until well blended. With the motor running, slowly pour in the oil through the feed tube until a thick mayonnaise forms. Add the lemon juice, mustard, tarragon, and salt and pepper to taste and process until smooth. Transfer to a nonmetallic bowl, cover with plastic wrap, and let chill until ready to serve.

Preheat the barbecue. Rinse the fish under cold running water and pat dry with paper towels. Mix the garlic, shallots, chili, and lemon juice together in a separate bowl. Rub the mixture onto both sides of the fillets.

Cook the fish over hot coals for 15 minutes, or until cooked through, turning once. Arrange the fish on a bed of salad greens, garnish with lemon wedges, and serve, with the aïoli and the vegetables for dipping served separately.

serves 6 | prep 15 minutes, plus 1 hour marinating | cook 16 minutes

INDONESIAN SPICED FISH

1–2 sea bream or red snapper, about
  2 lb 4 oz/1 kg
4 garlic cloves, finely chopped
2 fresh red chilies, seeded and
  finely chopped
1-inch/2.5-cm piece fresh gingerroot,
  thinly sliced
4 scallions, chopped
juice of 1 lime
2 tbsp corn oil, plus extra for brushing
salt
shredded coconut, to garnish
  (optional)

Clean the fish, then remove the scales, beginning at the tail and working toward the head. Rinse the fish inside and out under cold running water and pat dry with paper towels. Using a sharp knife, make a series of diagonal slashes on both sides of the fish. Put in a large, shallow, nonmetallic dish.

Put the garlic, chilies, ginger, and scallions in a food processor and process to a paste. Transfer to a small bowl, stir in the lime juice and oil, and season to taste with salt. Put 1–2 tablespoons of the spice mixture into the cavity of the fish and spoon the remainder over the fish, turning to coat. Cover with plastic wrap and let marinate in the refrigerator for up to 1 hour.

Preheat the barbecue. Lightly brush a fish basket with oil and put the fish in the basket. Set aside the marinade. Cook the fish over medium-hot coals, basting frequently with the reserved marinade, for 8 minutes on each side, or until the flesh flakes easily. Serve at once, garnished with coconut, if desired.

serves 4 | *prep* 10 minutes, plus 30 minutes' marinating | *cook* 10 minutes

TUNA & TARRAGON SKEWERS

10½ oz/300 g fresh tuna steaks
1 lb/450 g white mushrooms
chopped fresh tarragon, to garnish

MARINADE
2 tbsp white wine
3 tbsp balsamic vinegar
1 tbsp extra virgin olive oil
1 garlic clove, finely chopped
salt and pepper

TO SERVE
freshly cooked rice
mixed salad

If using wooden skewers, soak them in water for 30 minutes before using to prevent burning. Meanwhile, to make the marinade, put the wine, vinegar, olive oil, and garlic in a large bowl, season with salt and pepper to taste, and mix until well combined.

Rinse the tuna steaks under cold running water and pat dry with paper towels. Cut into small cubes. Thread the tuna cubes onto the skewers, alternating with the mushrooms. When the skewers are full (leave a small space at either end), transfer them to the bowl, and turn in the marinade until well coated. Cover with plastic wrap and let marinate in the refrigerator for at least 30 minutes.

Preheat the barbecue. Remove the skewers from the marinade and set aside the marinade. Cook the skewers over hot coals, turning frequently and basting with the reserved marinade, for 10 minutes, or until the tuna is cooked through (but do not overcook). Arrange the skewers on a bed of rice, garnish with chopped tarragon, and serve with a mixed salad.

serves 4 | *prep* 5 minutes, plus 1¹/₂ hours' marinating | *cook* 8 minutes

BARBECUED SWORDFISH

To make the marinade, put the rice wine, oil, garlic, lime juice, and cilantro in a bowl and mix until well combined.

Rinse the fish steaks under cold running water and pat dry with paper towels. Arrange the fish in a shallow, nonmetallic dish. Season to taste with salt and pepper, then pour over the marinade. Turn the fish in the marinade until well coated. Cover with plastic wrap and let marinate in the refrigerator for 1¹/₂ hours.

Preheat the barbecue. Remove the fish with a slotted spoon and set aside the marinade. Cook the fish over hot coals for 4 minutes. Turn the fish over, brush with the reserved marinade, and cook on the other side for an additional 4 minutes, or until cooked through.

Remove from the heat and garnish with chopped cilantro and lime slices. Serve with hot jacket baked potatoes, barbecued corncob, and a selection of salad greens.

4 swordfish steaks, about
   5¹/₂ oz/150 g each
salt and pepper
lime slices, to garnish

MARINADE
3 tbsp rice wine or sherry
3 tbsp chili oil
2 garlic cloves, finely chopped
juice of 1 lime
1 tbsp chopped fresh cilantro,
   plus extra to garnish

TO SERVE
freshly cooked jacket baked potatoes
barbecued corncob
selection of fresh salad greens

serves 6 | prep 20 minutes, plus 1 hour marinating | cook 6–8 minutes

STUFFED SARDINES

½ oz/15 g fresh parsley,
  finely chopped
4 garlic cloves, finely chopped
12 fresh sardines, cleaned
3 tbsp lemon juice
scant ⅔ cup all-purpose flour
1 tsp ground cumin
salt and pepper
olive oil, for brushing

Put the parsley and garlic in a bowl and mix together. Rinse the fish inside and out under cold running water and pat dry with paper towels. Spoon the herb mixture into the cavities of the fish and pat the remainder all over the outside of the fish. Sprinkle the sardines with lemon juice and transfer to a large, shallow, nonmetallic dish. Cover with plastic wrap and let marinate in the refrigerator for 1 hour.

Preheat the barbecue. Mix the flour and cumin together in a bowl, then season to taste with salt and pepper. Spread out the seasoned flour on a large, flat plate and gently roll the sardines in the seasoned flour to coat, then shake off any excess.

Brush the sardines with oil and cook over medium-hot coals for 3–4 minutes on each side. Serve at once.

serves 4 | prep 15 minutes | cook 10–16 minutes

BACON-WRAPPED TROUT

4 trout, cleaned
4 rindless smoked lean bacon slices
4 tbsp all-purpose flour
2 tbsp olive oil
2 tbsp lemon juice
salt and pepper
corn salad, to serve

TO GARNISH
fresh parsley sprigs
lemon wedges

Preheat the barbecue. Rinse the trout inside and out under cold running water and pat dry with paper towels. Stretch the bacon using the back of a heavy, flat-bladed knife.

Spread the flour out on a large, flat plate and season to taste with salt and pepper. Gently roll each trout in the seasoned flour until well coated, then shake off any excess. Beginning just below the head, wrap a bacon slice in a spiral along the length of each fish.

Brush the trout with oil and cook over medium hot coals for 5–8 minutes on each side. Transfer to 4 large serving plates and drizzle with the lemon juice. Garnish with parsley sprigs and lemon wedges and serve with corn salad.

serves 4 | prep 10 minutes, plus 30 minutes' marinating | cook 10 minutes

FENNEL-BASTED TROUT FILLETS

4 trout, cleaned and filleted
lemon wedges, to garnish

MARINADE
4 tsp vegetable oil
juice of ½ lemon
4 fresh fennel sprigs, finely chopped,
  plus extra sprigs to garnish
salt and pepper

To make the marinade, combine the oil
and lemon juice in a small bowl and whisk
together. Stir in the chopped fennel and salt
and pepper to taste.

Put the trout fillets in a shallow, nonmetallic
dish. Pour over the fennel mixture, cover the
dish with plastic wrap, and let marinate in
the refrigerator for 30 minutes.

Remove the trout from the refrigerator and
return to room temperature. Preheat the
griddle over medium heat. Transfer the trout
to the griddle and brush the marinade over
the fish. Cook the fillets for 5 minutes on each
side, turning once and brushing with the
remaining marinade.

Remove the trout from the griddle and
arrange on a serving dish. Garnish with
fennel sprigs and lemon wedges and
serve at once.

serves 4 | *prep 10 minutes, plus 1 hour marinating* | *cook 10–15 minutes*

WHOLE GRIDDLED FISH

4 tbsp chopped fresh mint
4 tbsp chopped fresh parsley
4 tbsp chopped fresh tarragon
4 trout, herring, or bass, cleaned and
    scaled, about 12 oz/350 g each
juice of 1 lemon
1 tbsp oil or butter, for brushing
4 tbsp butter, diced
salt and pepper

TO SERVE
freshly boiled new potatoes
green beans with almonds

Mix the herbs together in a small bowl. Put one-quarter of the mixture in the cavity of each fish, reserving a small amount for serving. Gently press the fish closed.

Make 2–3 shallow cuts on each side of the fish. Put the fish in a nonmetallic dish. Sprinkle with salt and pepper to taste and half the lemon juice. Rub in well. Cover the dish with plastic wrap and let marinate in the refrigerator for 1 hour.

Preheat the griddle over medium heat. Spray or brush with oil.

Dot the fish with half the diced butter, then put, buttered-side down, on the griddle. Cook for 6 minutes, or until the bottom is brown and crispy, then sprinkle the remaining lemon juice on top, dot with the remaining butter, and turn over to cook the second side.

Transfer the cooked fish to individual plates and serve with boiled new potatoes and green beans with almonds.

serves 4 | *prep* 15 minutes, plus 3–4 hour' marinating | *cook* 4–5 minutes

SHRIMP & MIXED PEPPER KABOBS

24 large raw shrimp, shelled and
deveined but with tails left intact
1 red bell pepper and 1 green bell
pepper, seeded and cut into
small chunks
lime wedges, to garnish
freshly cooked rice or Napa cabbage,
to serve

MARINADE
2 scallions, chopped
2 garlic cloves, finely chopped
1 fresh green chili and 1 small fresh
red chili, seeded and finely chopped
1 tbsp grated fresh gingerroot
1 tbsp snipped fresh chives
4 tbsp lime juice
1 tbsp finely grated lime rind
2 tbsp chili oil
salt and pepper

Put the scallions, garlic, chilies, ginger, chives, lime juice and rind, oil, and salt and pepper to taste in a food processor and process until smooth. Transfer to a nonmetallic bowl.

Thread the shrimp onto skewers, alternating with the red and green bell pepper chunks. If using wooden skewers soak them in water for 30 minutes before using to prevent burning. When the skewers are full (leave a small space at either end), transfer to the bowl, and turn in the marinade until well coated. Cover with plastic wrap and let marinate in the refrigerator for 3–4 hours.

Preheat the barbecue. Remove the kabobs from the marinade and set aside the marinade. Cook the kabobs over hot coals, turning frequently and basting with the reserved marinade, for 4–5 minutes, or until the shrimp are cooked through (but do not overcook). Arrange the skewers on a bed of rice or Napa cabbage, garnish with lime wedges, and serve.

serves 4 | prep 5 minutes | cook 10–15 minutes

SEAFOOD BROCHETTES

4 live scallops, shucked and cleaned
4 baby squid, cleaned
4 raw jumbo shrimp, in their shells
4 white mushrooms
4 cherry tomatoes
4 baby corn (optional)
2 tbsp vegetable oil, for basting
few flat-leaf parsley sprigs, to garnish
buttered rice, to serve

Select skewers that will fit on your griddle. If using wooden skewers, soak them in water for 30 minutes before using to prevent burning. Preheat the griddle over medium heat.

Meanwhile, thread several pieces of all 3 types of seafood and the vegetables alternately onto each skewer.

Put the kabobs on the griddle and cook, turning frequently and basting occasionally with oil, for 5–10 minutes, or until the fish is firm and the vegetables are tender. Be careful not to overcook the squid, or it will be tough.

Remove the kabobs from the griddle and transfer to individual serving plates. Garnish with parsley and serve with buttered rice.

INDEX

aïoli 46, 239
American plaice 17
anchovies 24
    bagna cauda 62
    devils on horseback 63
    green sauce 197
    linguine 157
    pan bagna 146
    pissaladière 156
    salade niçoise 173
angler fish 20
    blackened 235
    deep-fried seafood 149
    fish curry 204
    in fish soup 105, 106, 121
    kabobs 238
    Louisiana gumbo 130
    packages 203
    rosemary and bacon
        skewers 86

baking 41
barbecuing 40, 41
barracuda 21
bass see sea bass
bays 26
béchamel sauce 45
beurre blanc 47
braising 41
bread, pan bagna 146
brill 17
broiling 40
burritos 152
buying fish 14

calamares 99
catfish 25
ceviche 92
char 25
choosing fish 14

clams 26
    Brazilian seafood stew 133
    buying 14
    Catalan fish stew 131
    New England clam chowder
        124
    preparing 37
    seafood risotto 165
    spaghetti 163

coalfish 19
cod 19
    Brazilian seafood stew 133
    burritos 152
    Catalan fish stew 131
    with Catalan spinach 201
    cioppino 122
    fish cakes 147
    fish curry 204
    in fish soup 105, 106
    flaky pastry fish pie 202
    Louisiana gumbo 130
    smoked, chowder 116
    with spinach 201
    stew with celery and potatoes
        127
    and sweet potato soup 102
    tacos 150
    Thai fish cakes 83
    and tomato packages 234
    tostadas with salsa 151
    and yogurt quenelles 153
coley 19
cooking methods 38–41
court bouillon 44
couscous, Moroccan salad 174
crab 27
    Brazilian seafood stew 133
    and cantaloupe salad 191
    Caribbean crab cakes 73

choosing 14
    and citrus salsa 189
    crispy won tons 75
    potted 96
    preparing 34
    seafood phyllo packages 74
    soufflé 167
    and corn soup 114
    and watercress tart 166
crayfish/crawfish 27

deep-frying 38
dolphin fish/dorado 18
Dover sole 17, 32
drum 23
Dublin Bay prawn 27

eels 24, 25
English sole 17, 149

filleting fish 30, 31, 32
fish cakes 73, 83, 147
fish curry, with noodles 204
fish directory 16–27
fisherman's pie 216
fish fritters 60
fish pie, flaky pastry 202
fish soup
    bouillabaisse 121
    Breton 105
    cioppino 122
    garlic 104
    Mexican 107
    saffron 106
fish stock 44, 108
flatfish 16, 17–18, 28, 29, 30–1
flounder 17, 207, 216
freshwater fish 25
frozen fish 14, 15